# THE
# PHILOSOPHY OF AMERICAN
# DEMOCRACY

# THE
# PHILOSOPHY OF AMERICAN
# DEMOCRACY

*Edited by*

## CHARNER M. PERRY

KENNIKAT PRESS
Port Washington, N. Y./London

THE PHILOSOPHY OF AMERICAN DEMOCRACY

Copyright 1943 by the University of Chicago Press
Reissued in 1971 by Kennikat Press by arrangement
with the University of Chicago Press
Library of Congress Catalog Card No: 71-132089
ISBN 0-8046-1417-2

Manufactured by Taylor Publishing Company     Dallas, Texas

ESSAY AND GENERAL LITERATURE INDEX REPRINT SERIES

# FOREWORD

✻

LECTURES given at the University of Chicago under the Charles R. Walgreen Foundation for the Study of American Institutions are designed to assist students toward an understanding of contemporary life in the United States—its background in history, its ideals, values, and institutions, its present needs and possible future. To foster an intelligent citizenship and patriotism, not narrowly nationalistic in their expression, and with thought and knowledge much more than emotion as their foundation, is a principal purpose of this Foundation.

The substance of the essays in this volume was given in lectures to audiences of students during the spring of 1942. Now in revised and extended form they are published with the hope that they may be of service to many readers beyond the limits of the University of Chicago campus. They are the last of the three Walgreen Foundation series of the academic year 1941–42. The other two, already in print, are entitled *Religion and the Present Crisis* and *Economic Problems of War and Its Aftermath.* The present volume, like these others, is sponsored by the Walgreen Foundation, but its publication has depended above all upon the generous co-operation of the authors, the editor, and the University of Chicago Press.

WILLIAM T. HUTCHINSON

*Executive Secretary, Charles R. Walgreen Foundation
for the Study of American Institutions*

# INTRODUCTION

## CHARNER PERRY

✢

IN THESE troubled days when all our institutions and habitual ways are warped and changed by the needs of war, we hope that when victory is won we shall restore normal conditions and return to the life we knew before the war. We know, nevertheless, that not all things can be again exactly as they were, nor do we wish to duplicate the mistakes, the completed undertakings, or the trivia of a lost world. We do not wish to repeat unchanged the hectic and unsteady boom of the twenties or the painful depression of the thirties. What we want is to restore the framework of our past lives— the essential institutions and fundamental principles that constitute American democracy.

Historians today still attempt to see just what was essential to the Roman Empire and then to trace the changes that led to its dissolution. We may be sure that the Romans, taken up with projects that were momentarily important and lost in the day-to-day tangle of events, had but the haziest notion of the institutions basic to Roman strength. We know that there were orators who complained of some trivial departure from custom that the very foundations of the republic were being undermined, and we know that there were politicians who while setting in train disastrous sequences of events proclaimed that their policies were interwoven indistinguishably with the fabric of the Roman state.

Perhaps we understand our society better than the Romans understood theirs; but a sober look at the evidence is not reassuring. Without attempting to run over the evidence, one may point to obviously pertinent facts. In recent years many New Deal measures have been vigorously attacked and as vigorously defended on the ground that they contravene or carry out fundamental principles of American democracy. No matter how bitter the conflict, both sides have claimed to speak for the American way of life. Usually there have been three or four sides rather than two, each of them presenting its own plausible interpretation of the main drift of America. It may well be that future historians will find that our orators and politicians fretted about surface trivialities or irrelevant issues while our country developed, and perhaps later declined, as the result of the actions of citizens taken up with immediate problems and unaware of the far-off results of their day-to-day decisions.

The establishment of the Walgreen Foundation to promote the understanding of American institutions has turned out to be a remarkably timely act of wisdom. The lecture series and the published volumes sponsored by the Foundation provide an invaluable occasion for study of matters urgently demanding our attention.

If we are to have assurance of returning to pre-war America we must find our way through the oratory, the propaganda, and the sea of plausible prophecies to an apprehension of the keystone structure of our democracy. How to return to our pre-war institutions is, however, only one, and perhaps the lesser, of two problems. It seems that whether we wish it or not we have and shall have an important influence in the reshaping of world political structure. To guide this influence we must turn to our own experience. There is no other possibility open to us; but even if there were we might justifiably feel that our American political experience has been sufficiently successful to serve, not as a pattern for other countries, but as a rich source of wisdom to be made available for the solution of world problems. The unpleasant fact is, however, that applications of American principles to international problems are as various and as confusing as their applications to domestic issues. Difficulties arise, no doubt, from the complexity of things international in scale and from our ignorance of some of the factors involved; but one suspects that the major difficulty is our ignorance of our own intrinsic pattern, our failure to grasp the underlying organization and the vital rationale developed in American political struggles. If we could see clearly the reasons why America has been a good place in which to live—not merely the goods we so obviously enjoy, but the hidden machinery, the intricate network of customs, ideals, and institutions upon which they depend—then we could with more confidence guess how other countries might be m.de better.

The essays in this volume approach the task from various points, but all of them aim at the problem indicated above: What are the essential features of American democracy? In view of the size and difficulty of the problem it would be foolish to claim that this volume gives or attempts a complete solution; but I may assert with confidence that it contains insights which raise it above the level of the usual discussions of the topic, and which will be of great value to the citizen attempting to see the real America through the fog of current events.

In view of the diverse interests and backgrounds of the contributors it is surprising that something like a recurrent theme in various forms should appear in the essays; and since the theme is not one of the familiar commonplaces, and even runs counter to our usual beliefs, there is the more occasion for surprise.

To put the matter with a bluntness which may seem shocking, particularly to some of the authors, each of the contributors seems to feel that whatever the basis of democratic government it is not justice and right. None of them defends injustice and unrighteousness, and each of them is convinced that American political institutions have been outstandingly successful in achieving justice and right. Nonetheless, they seem deeply convinced that it is a mistake for government or citizens to pursue justice too closely, and folly to believe that our national and international problems can be solved merely by deciding what is right and pushing for it at all costs. This is one rendering of the joint solicitude felt particularly by Knight and Smith over the romanticism which they find to characterize the democratic faith. Perhaps there is a paradox or perplexing subtlety here; but, since my purpose is merely to call attention to the point, I need not attempt a full and clear statement.

Dean Faust concerns himself with matters of history; but the moral of his story seems to be that statesmen should, like the Founding Fathers, see that their problem is not to work out an ideal scheme and then to force it on the country, but rather to devise a scheme which will leave most matters of right and deep conviction unsettled but which will have two indispensable characteristics: it will meet the needs of common action and it will be such that most men can be persuaded from interest or from conviction to accept it. It will be acceptable to most people precisely because it represents no man's conviction as to what is exactly right and just.

The story which Professor Smith tells of Tom Paine seems to have somewhere in it much the same moral. A man who, like Tom Paine, knows what is right and wrong (particularly what is wrong) and is passionately moved by his convictions may be useful in a revolution—and perhaps a progressive country should always have a small revolutionary fringe—but in the construction and running of a government he would be an impossible obstructionist.

In Professor Knight's complex analysis the indicated theme

is not so prominent, but nevertheless it is there. His emphasis upon the unreconciled conflicts among our ideals, upon our reluctance to consider how much one ideal will cost in the sacrifice of other ideals, and upon unconstrained agreement as the essential condition for free or democratic co-operation points to a preoccupation with the same problems, if not a commitment to exactly the same doctrines, as appear in the other essays.

Perhaps an interpretation of American institutions could begin as well from some other point, but it is surprising how the theme appearing in these essays leads, when carefully considered, to other basic principles, and how use of it as a point of reference helps to bring characteristic traits of the American tradition into relation with each other.

Let us consider briefly several frequently mentioned traits of American government. It has been said that we live under a system of law, rather than under a system of personal decision or arbitrary administrative action. It is said that we have freedom and a system of free enterprise rather than paternalism or regimentation. It is said that we have government by the people, with governmental action reflecting the public will and depending upon the consent of the governed. These, surely, are basic factors of our political order—but consider them in relation to each other and in relation to the theme prominent in these essays.

An essential characteristic of laws is their generality. They are the same for everyone, and they set up a general framework within which individuals and groups make their own decisions and plans. The other side of the same fact is that most matters that are important and upon which we have deep convictions are not settled by governmental action, at least not in peacetime. In wartime, when the government must decide which men shall be called to the army, who shall have new tires, how commodities shall be distributed, we see that our system of laws, while not discarded, is quite inadequate to the burdens of government and must be supplemented by vast administrative and bureaucratic machinery.

Freedom and the system of free enterprise are complementary to the system of law. A large part of our freedom consists in the fact that government does not make decisions in detail but furnishes merely a structure within which individual decisions may be made; but in a complex society individual decisions are integrated into orderly co-operation through the system of free enterprise, or the market. As Professor Knight emphasizes, the market does not always give us what we should have or everything that we want. Nevertheless, law, freedom, and free markets are so closely interwoven that one should consider long before attempting to separate them.

It might be contended that law, freedom, and free enterprise are all secondary—that all of these might be lost and yet a government be democratic if it reflected the will of the people and rested upon the consent of the governed. There is some merit in this contention; but it is doubtful whether consent of the governed can long be secure or significant in the absence of the other conditions. Two questions may be posed by reference to present wartime conditions. We all want to win the war, and, since we have confidence in the ability and good intentions of most of our elected officials, we tend to accept governmental decisions with good grace. The truth is, however, that the public is not able to judge policies except in their broadest outlines and that consequently we must to a great extent simply take governmental and administrative decisions for the time being on faith. This is necessary and therefore right in an emergency—but if war or war conditions were indefinitely prolonged and we indefinitely took governmental decisions on faith, then consent of the governed would be indistinguishable from the acquiescence of any governed people. The second question may be posed by reminding ourselves that today we are all united in evaluating any policy by its relation to the one end of winning the war—but suppose that the war is won and we have returned to our peacetime diversity of interests and convictions. To what extent could we reach agreement and consequently general consent upon detailed decisions —which religion is right, what children should go to college, which people should have new automobiles, and all the other matters that have traditionally been outside the sphere of governmental decision?

One may doubt that men could construct and maintain a system of government unless most of them accepted certain minimum ideals, and we know that if we could reach fuller agreement on fundamental matters we could proceed further and more effectively in our national undertakings. The fact remains, however, that in America we have not had and do not at the moment foresee any general agreement as to what is right and just. We do not have a ruling class made like minded by a common tradition or an identical education. We have groups with diverse backgrounds, interests, habits, and convictions. Surely, we may wonder why we have not fallen apart into dozens of bickering states or irreconcilable factions brought into uneasy peace only by violent dictatorships. In view of all the handicaps and the possible causes of conflict, the American nation stands out in the long history of human strife as an astonishing success in co-operation and the maintenance of order. If we can see why we have not fallen, at least not permanently, into ever threatening conflict, then we can hope in the future to avoid such disaster, and we may even with some confidence offer our experience to a disordered world.

In these essays—which, as I have indicated, are preoccupied with the problem of attaining co-operation in the absence of agreement as to what is right—there is a contribution to an understanding of the American experiment and what it may have to offer in the solution of international problems.

# TABLE OF CONTENTS

✿

# I

# THOMAS PAINE: VOICE OF DEMOCRATIC REVOLUTION

## T. V. SMITH

✳

If systems of government can be introduced less expensive and more productive of general happiness than those which have existed, all attempts to oppose their progress will in the end be fruitless. Reason, like time, will make its own way, and prejudice will fall in a combat with interest. If universal peace, civilization, and commerce are ever to be the happy lot of man, it cannot be accomplished but by a revolution in the system of governments.—THOMAS PAINE, *The Rights of Man.*

DEMOCRACY is a doctrine of revolution. Come the revolution, however, democracy passes, if it is to be preserved, into the practice of evolution. A chronic revolutionary is a paradox, and permanent revolution would be anarchy. In the division of civic labor, however, some men can be revolutionary all the time and some men evolutionary all the time, but not all men either any of the time. Historically, it does appear that democracy must be revolutionary to begin with, because men are animals and will not choose between evils until one of the evils becomes so intolerable as to provoke revolt. Democracy is evolutionary to end with, because men are spirits and seek to perfect the good in any mixed evil which they have been forced to choose. As in most good things, there is in democracy, then, a strange mixture of the gradual and the precipitate. The evolutionary phase of grad-

1

ualism can be made inclusive of the precipitate phase of revolution: democracy-in-action has well been called "the institu-
tionalization of the principle of revolution."

In discussing the genius of democratic government and in
celebrating the virtue of the democratic way of life, I propose
to keep your feet on the ground, however much my own head
may soar to the empyrean. This I shall do for you by fixating
attention initially upon Thomas Paine, the most stirring voice
of modern democracy in revolution; and, eventually, upon
Justice Oliver Wendell Holmes, the sagest voice of democracy
in evolution. While you attend to these Americans and pa-
triots—escaping thus the fate of those who, as the American
poet says, "would not listen to their voices"[1]—I shall weave
around these personages, if not deduce from them, a philosophy of democracy ambivalent enough to accommodate itself
to both war (*revolution*) and peace (*evolution*).

The ambivalence is clearly indicated, even if by all good
men deprecated; for a clarity of explanation (such as dialecti-
cians practice) that is much clearer than what is explained is
hardly to be recommended to the naïve as key to dynamic institutions. No collective agency can with truth be rendered
unequivocally honorific. A democracy that cannot win at
war is already decadent for an age as martial as this one, and a
democracy that cannot make and maintain peace that is progressive (which, that is, does not each decade transcend the
deadness of the decade before) loses its soul in seeking to save
it. Let me preface, then, what I shall further say by this
duplex overtone for democracy dynamic: *A collective enterprise
in which (for war) you may kick or even kill other men without de-
spising them, and in which (for peace) you may deeply dislike some
men without kicking or even wishing to kick them.* Such ambivalence betokens toughness enough to wage war successfully and

[1] Edwin Arlington Robinson, *The Glory of the Nightingales* (New York: Mac-
millan Co., 1930).

tolerance enough to abide patiently the best peace (always bad enough) that can be made. Thus do we make room in democracy—as, of course, we must, to escape self-frustrating romanticism—for the tactics of malevolence no less than for a strategy of benevolence. Whether we approach our subject from the standpoint of liberty, as Professor Knight does herein, or from the vantage of equality, as I have heretofore (*American Philosophy of Equality; Democratic Way of Life; Beyond Conscience*), we safeguard ourselves against disillusion by remembering that the metaphysics of democracy is a most mixed business—no business, indeed, for either the lazy or the simple-minded.

### I. PAINE: THE MODEL REVOLUTIONARY

Thomas Paine, writing at our national beginning, declares in *Common Sense* that government is a "mode" of control "rendered necessary by the inability of moral virtue to govern the world."[2] Since the very fact of government thus advertises a moral letdown if not breakdown, it is always bad. At its worst, indeed, government is an intolerable evil, as he says, and at its best is but a "necessary evil."[3] Here is a truth more profound than the elegance of its eighteenth-century dress suggests. Children may cry when their choice is other than between two sweets; adolescents may complain when the choice is between an evil and a bare good; but adults must learn not to repine or even hesitate when the choice is between evils. Such choice the adult will make from the prudence which, as Paine says, "in every case advises him, out of two evils, to choose the least."[4]

Paine's philosophy, as befits a revolutionary, is simple; but

[2] Quotations will be credited to Paine's separate works, but will for convenience be taken from, and paginated under, *The Writings of Thomas Paine* ("Modern Library," edited with an introduction by Carl Van Doren [New York: Boni & Liveright, 1922]). *Common Sense*, p. 4.

[3] *Ibid.*, p. 1.      [4] *Ibid.*, p. 2.

it is adequate to enable him to distinguish between society, a good permitting choices between goods, and government, an evil compelling choices between evils. Paine is, indeed, proud of the simplicity of his philosophy. He elevates its virtue into what he calls "a principle in nature"—a principle "which no art can overturn, viz. that the more simple anything is, the less liable it is to be disordered, and the easier repaired when disordered."[5]

This pride in the simple makes it clear from the outset that from this man Paine derives a democratic apologetics that counsels us to seek the citadel of virtue by turning our backs upon complexities and collectivities. Social groups are as superior to government as is a choice between goods *and* evils superior to a choice between evils. The individual is as superior to social groupings as a choice between goods is superior to a choice between evils *and* goods. Pursue the path away from the collective, and you are on your way to a domain in which "the impulses of conscience are clear, uniform"— though, alas, as he adds, not irresistibly obeyed.[6] Pursue the path through society to government, and you are confessing the inability of moral virtue to be the dominant principle of collective action. The Founding Fathers had a harder task than this, as Dean Faust herein shows.

It is this degradation of the ideal which no revolutionary can suffer in silence. Revolution is of the heart before it is of the head. Paine is no exception to this generalization. He could no more keep still in the moving presence of what seemed to him dead wrong than he could assess the (dis)utility of his speaking his mind. A man who could, from exile in France, write a letter of cumulative insults to the idol of a nation, as Paine did to President Washington, in hope of sympathy from that idol and assistance from that nation, was not a man in whom reason was an adequate "scout" for the pas-

[5] *Ibid.*, p. 4.          [6] *Ibid.*, p. 2.

sions, as Hume in the name of the Enlightenment prescribed for the children of the Enlightenment.

A further word upon the general nature of the revolutionary —and upon democracy as revolution—is in order before we settle to a summary of Paine's own philosophy. We have already descried in the revolutionary a discrepancy between feeling and reason. There is a larger discrepancy between visions of the ideal and any adequate grasp of stark realities.

Always, alas, there is a yawning gap between what "ought to be" and what at any time "is." Revolution does not arise merely from this cosmic yawn; if so, mankind would be in a constant state of violent rebellion against both fellow-men and Mother Nature herself. There must arise a human feeling of this cosmic discrepancy, weighting the scales until revulsion seems the only fit response to any status quo.

That is to put the matter negatively. The revolutionary is also a man of affirmation—more affirmative, indeed, than his enemies are ever likely to admit. He sees ideals clearly, he takes them seriously, he apprentices himself to them as for the time more real than the factualities of the given status quo. Habits keep other men in line with custom. The revolutionary is short on habits and long on ideals. Men well armored with the use and wont of the world can admit that things are, of course, not as they ought to be, without doing much if anything about it. But a man long enough on lovely ideals and short enough on stable habits is budged into action out of direct deference to ideals so clearly discerned.

In all which this analysis implies, Thomas Paine was a true and model revolutionary. He was Shelley's West Wind, before whose incarnated

> . . . . presence the leaves dead
> Are driven like ghosts from an enchanter fleeing—

an incarnated but unattached West Wind, driving

> . . . . dead thoughts over the universe,
> Like withered leaves, to quicken a new birth. . . . .

Even domestic discipline, effective in tying many men to stable ways, was fragile in Paine's case, broken once by death, once by marital separation.  And the larger discipline of patriotism, which prescribes an orbit at least for other men, could not catch and hold this waif of the wind,

Wild Spirit . . . . moving everywhere!

For a fact, Paine's roots were never deep in any national soil.  Indeed, for most of his life it was a matter of animated controversy as to which of three countries could with greatest show of reason claim the honor, if it was an honor, of his citizenship.  He left his native England voluntarily but more hurriedly than the prosperous approved.  But he did not more flee the state of a debtor than pursue the dream of a better world unfolded to him by Benjamin Franklin, then in London.  After helping rhetorically to engineer a revolution against his native land, he returned to the land he had rebuffed to make his fortune in exploiting an iron bridge which he had invented —returned, however, as the sequel had it, only to begin a revolutionary movement there.  Presently outlawed in England, he escaped the sheriff by an hour of darkness and an inch of his own coattail.

Welcomed then to France as a revolutionary by the Revolution, he was elected deputy for Versailles as well as for Calais, only at last to be imprisoned as a "foreigner" and kept imprisoned a whole year as an Englishman because, as it appears, the American minister, Gouverneur Morris, would not ask his release as an American citizen. Released at last, when Monroe, succeeding Morris, did claim his citizenship American, Paine returned to America, at length to be denied the right to vote in his own precinct (New Rochelle) on the ground that he was not an American citizen.

Perhaps he was not an American citizen, though he was a founding father of American citizenship.  Perhaps he was not a French citizen, though he contributed mightily to the freedom on which that citizenship was to rest. Perhaps he was not an Englishman, though he was born in England and never ceased to loose his tongue to lash for her perfection. Certain it is that his loyalty, wherever it belonged, was incarnate citizenship, however much on the loose. "Where liberty is *not*," he corrected Franklin, "there is my home." His homeland *was* Liberty itself; he was but absent in America, in France, in England—absent on leave from his homeland of Ideal Liberty. No revolution did ever succeed, or perhaps could ever have succeeded, well enough to justify Paine in taking out second papers for mundane citizenship. By the time he took out first papers, his revolution would always be enough awry to justify his moving on.

*Come the revolution, betrayed is the revolution.* "Certainly . . . .," rejoins Carl Becker, the historian. "It is in the nature of revolutions to be betrayed, since life and history have an inveterate habit of betraying the aspirations of men." Even democratic government, always and everywhere, as Becker concludes, "has been so far betrayed, the ideal so imperfectly portrayed in the course of events, that the conditions essential to the practice of its virtues are not easily noted."[7]

Paine was a revolutionist who could never become an evolutionist. Fortunately for him and others, Paine was not in the Constitutional Convention. Time was too short and ideals both too precious and too pressing to permit of his gradualism. And to his ardent spirit those who did become gradualists were themselves betraying the revolution. It was this which Paine really had against Washington, in the (in)famous letter previously referred to: Washington had to count the cost of violence and heal the wounds already inflicted by revolution. Paine would have nothing of this; no revolution was to him a success which did not breed a revolution against itself. This

[7] *New Liberties for Old* (New Haven: Yale University Press, 1941), p. 103.

was not, however, because Paine favored violence for its own sake, as is the case with certain contemporary revolutionists, who boast that chronic violence alone is "dynamic." Paine was not devoted to violence; as a Quaker he tolerated it only as a last resort. He counseled exile (in America) rather than death for Louis XVI. It was in Paine's case, the rather, because he served only the ideal with no continuing obeisance to the realities through which the ideal comes to birth and with small patience for the limits prescribed to the ideal by action. Paine's instinct was generous, as is the instinct of many a revolutionary; but Paine's patience was short, as is revolutionary patience everywhere. Any man who somehow thinks that action, any action, can completely fulfil the ideal, any ideal, will always be in trouble; and if he lacks patience to abide his troubles, he will always keep other men in trouble. He is the true revolutionist, I now repeat—he who is long on ideals, short on habits, and pithy with impatience. Such was Thomas Paine, the voice of American democracy in initial revolution.

Corrective of this revolutionary temperament of "all or none"—a temperament patient, as Paine put it, at seeing "precedents . . . . taken in a lump"[8]—America was fortunate in having early and in keeping until late the type of patriotism also which can content itself with "some and some," some evolution and some revolution all along. I have spoken of Washington as belonging to such a type. A better example still was Jefferson, believing in evolution as a policy, in revolution as strategy; tolerant of his dearest enemies like Hamilton, patient of obvious wrongs like slavery, Jefferson was confident that the prod of revolutionary prowess every nineteen years or so would make patience meantime more productive of progress. But this was a phase of democracy yet to come when Paine prodded the crisis into violence. They also serve

[8] *Rights of Man*, p. 161.

democracy who only poke and prod. With this homely thought to guide us, let us turn now to the type of revolutionary philosophy which made Paine one of the greatest voices of democracy as revolutionary leaven.

## II. A SUMMARY VIEW OF PAINE'S PHILOSOPHY

Paine invented little if anything ideological. He did, however, turn to the account of action ideas of other men and the major increments of our cultural inheritance. And his contribution was not merely negative. True, his sledge-hammer blows against irresponsible monarchy as alternative to democracy were certainly calculated to enlist prudence against as well as destroy nostalgia for the government which American tories tolerated.

While Paine's temperament could never fully stomach the fruits of action, especially the more faulty fruits of collective action, his chief service was in prodding other men into action. This service necessitates and justifies resort to platitudes, because they are the certainties of the people. To render certitude into certainty through impetuosity—this is the task of the revolutionary if he is to escape the scaffold and erect the dais of a new order. These certitudes which Paine seized upon may be set down summarily as (1) the rights of men as men, natural in origin and moral in demand; (2) the monopoly of these rights by one side, his side; (3) the disregard and at length the denial by the other side of this monopoly of virtue by his side; and, finally, (4) the evil nature even if necessary existence of government.

### NATURAL RIGHTS RATHER THAN NATURAL LAW

Let us make three observations upon these certitudes which Paine labored mightily and successfully to turn into the certainty always felt by men on the march. This first observation is that his concern was with natural rights rather than with natural law. While there is much to be said about natural law as basis for revolution, Paine made it his business to say little of it. Leave that to the philosophers. Paine was a philosophic revolutionary, not a speculative philosopher; and it is the first business, though not the last business, of a philosopher of revolution to understand this preference for action over reflection as itself constituting the major item in the philosophy of any revolutionist. Negatively, this preference concerns the way in which inaction is rendered intolerable; positively, the way in which action is rendered desirable. One way to render inaction intolerable is to superinduce the easy conviction that (2) men have a monopoly upon virtue, and doubly well done is this task when men are convinced (3) that the wrong done them is done them by inferiors. This is at once "to abuse the plaintiff," to elevate the defendant, and at last to change the venue from forbearance to intolerance.

At this whole jumbled process Paine was superb. The colonists knew that they were being wronged. Was not taxation, always an injury, being made an insult through lack of representation? Decent men were being wronged, as Paine put it, by a system which "watches prosperity as its prey and permits none to escape without a tribute."[9] They were being wronged, yes; but to the cautious, some wrong is inevitable, and some wrong not inevitable is not worth rebelling against, and wrong not inevitable and even not worth rebelling against may with patience be corrected less expensively than through revolution. Thus the conservative temperament. These doubts countenancing inaction could all be best resolved for revolutionary action by showing how rotten was the institution of monarchy which afflicted decent men, how glorious the democratic vistas before them. To both ends, but particularly to the negative one, Paine hurled, therefore, his heaviest thunderbolts. They are bolts that reverberate in

[9] *Ibid.*, p. 151.

democratic ears even to this day. Hear again the echoes of their crashings.

In origin, monarchy is "nothing better than the principal ruffian of some restless gang."[10] In perpetuity, it stands, as in origin, not for peace but for war: "Britain, for centuries past, has been nearly fifty years out of every hundred at war with some power or other."[11] In succession, it represents always the imposition of moral mediocrity and often of dynastic idiocy upon the wise and the good: "it opens a door to the *foolish*, the *wicked*, and the *improper*."[12] Such as these rule, out of the impudent conceit of their own superiority. From such premises what conclusions follow? What conclusions could follow? In Paine's own barbed and piercing words: "Of more worth is one honest man to society, and in the sight of God, than all the crowned ruffians that ever lived."[13] And, more specifically, this follows: "I cannot see on what grounds the king of Britain can look up to heaven for help against us: a common murderer, a highwayman, or a housebreaker, has as good a pretence as he."[14]

As to the aristocracy surrounding and supporting such monarchy, this conclusion: "The first aristocrats in all countries were brigands. Those of later times, sycophants."[15] As for himself, Paine notes this conclusion: "I should suffer the misery of devils, were I to make a whore of my soul by swearing allegiance to one whose character is that of a sottish, stupid, stubborn, worthless, brutish man."[16] Strong words those, but all effectively calculated to make conversational certitudes into certainties for revolutionary action.

For those not sharing such certitudes to begin with, Paine links analysis with odium and prudence with menace. All

[10] *Common Sense*, p. 14.
[11] *The American Crisis*, p. 63.
[12] *Common Sense*, p. 16.
[13] *Ibid.*, p. 19.
[14] *The American Crisis*, p. 42.
[15] *Rights of Man*, p. 175.
[16] *The American Crisis*, p. 49.

hesitant ones he puts into four classes: "interested men, who are not to be trusted, weak men who *cannot* see, prejudiced men who will not see, and a certain set of moderate men who think better of the European world than it deserves; and this last class, by an ill-judged deliberation, will be the cause of more calamities to this Continent than all the other three."[17] Proposing expropriation of recalcitrant tories, so that tainted money might be untainted through this process of advantageous purging, Paine honors the revolution which he has provoked with the immortal invocation to action pronounced at Valley Forge: "These are the times that try men's souls. The summer soldier and the sunshine patriot will, in this crisis, shrink from the service of their country; but he that stands it now, deserves the love and thanks of man and woman."[18]

No new facts of science there, you say. No, none—Paine was the voice of revolution. All rhetoric, you say, including most of the "facts." Yes, indeed—Paine was the voice of revolution. As Jefferson remarked in defense of the unoriginality of the Declaration of Independence: he did not suppose himself called upon to formulate a new philosophy, but only to make applicable for action the philosophy men already had. Revolution is always a call to action, and action that is resolute must escape the equivocality characteristic of all honest debate. It pays wise men to remember—however semanticists forget—that language arose in action and exists as much for the sake of provoking action as for the purpose of communicating truth. Outside of purely intellectual circles, the one function of language is as important as the other, and each indispensable in turn—not to mention still a third function, that of mere enjoyment. Certainly rhetoric, in its turn, is a mighty stimulant to the juices of revolution and a sedative

[17] *Common Sense*, pp. 26–27.
[18] *The American Crisis*, p. 41.

not to be smiled at as the democratic impetus passes into its evolutionary phase. Paine was a powerful voice to turn group certitudes into universal certainty such as resolute action requires. The available doctrine of natural rights was put to this account, and the only natural law which Paine needed to support obvious right against more obvious wrong was the indigenous moral law of every conscience—that *it is not right to endure insufferable wrongs*. There may be philosophy more profound than that, but hardly a basis of action more secure.

### NATURAL RIGHTS AS SELF-EVIDENT MORAL CLAIMS

There is, however, a second observation that should be made upon Paine's use of natural rights. I refer now to the content given that term by Paine. Alternative as such "rights" are to overt wrong, Paine's natural rights appear more circumspect than Locke's and less so than Jefferson's. Locke's, it will be recalled, were "life, liberty and property." Jefferson's were "life, liberty and the pursuit of happiness." Paine's leaned to Locke's in form, but in meaning to Jefferson's. Locke had rationalized a revolution already consummated, and a bloodless revolution at that. Jefferson was rationalizing a bloody revolution to be made, and made by many fighters who as yet had little property of their own. So property and other means of happiness were to them more a pursuit than a possession. Property was for Jefferson a right to be established and properly generalized through the revolution, but not a right laid down by nature herself. Jefferson's conception of natural rights was realistic: natural rights end where individual powers cease.

Paine himself is not oblivious to this distinction between competence and claim (a distinction which Professor Knight is presently to elucidate). Both categories of rights, however —what men have and what they ought to have—he calls "natural"; only civil rights must be added to natural rights, like property, to implement them. To Paine, natural rights are moral, existing irrespective of the power to enjoy. To Jefferson rights are not natural if men lack individually the power to enter upon their appropriation. But hear Paine's own pregnant words upon this point:

Natural rights are those which appertain to man in right of his existence. Of this kind are all the intellectual rights, or rights of the mind, and also all those rights of acting as an individual for his own comfort and happiness, which are not injurious to the natural rights of others. Civil rights are those which appertain to man in right of his being a member of society. Every civil right has for its foundation some natural right pre-existing in the individual, but to the enjoyment of which his individual power is not, in all cases, sufficiently competent. Of this kind are all those which relate to security and protection. [Here would come property.][19]

Where individual power ends, there natural rights end, save as natural rights are transmuted into (Paine says "exchanged for") civil rights.

In Paine's case, natural rights that exist but are inoperative through individual incompetence are made effective through social competence under the head of civil rights. There exists for men a higher right to make all natural rights effective through pooling their resources, but the unearned increment of power arising from the pool cannot be used to invalidate any natural right. This guarantees the individual in perpetuity, and that in spite of his weakness, making the state never his end but only his standard means for the pursuit of happiness.

While Paine's poetry is not thought by poets to bear quoting, a philosopher may venture one of Paine's ditties (written in 1775) for the sake of a fine figure for future use:

[19] *Rights of Man*, p. 133.

## LIBERTY TREE

In a chariot of light from the regions of day,
   The Goddess of Liberty came;
Ten thousand celestials directed the way,
   And hither conducted the dame.
A fair budding branch from the gardens above,
   Where millions with millions agree,
She brought in her hand as a pledge of her love,
   And the plant she named *Liberty Tree*.

The celestial exotic struck deep in the ground,
   Like a native it flourished and bore;
The fame of its fruit drew the nations around,
   To seek out this peaceable shore.
Unmindful of names or distinctions they came,
   For freemen like brothers agree;
With one spirit endued, they one friendship pursued,
   And their temple was *Liberty Tree*.

Beneath this fair tree, like the patriarchs of old,
   Their bread in contentment they ate,
Unvexed with the troubles of silver and gold,
   The cares of the grand and the great.
With timber and tar they Old England supplied,
   And supported her power on the sea;
Her battles they fought, without getting a groat,
   For the honor of *Liberty Tree*.

But hear, O ye swains, 'tis a tale most profane,
   How all the tyrannical powers,
Kings, Commons and Lords, are uniting amain,
   To cut down this guardian of ours;
From the east to the west blow the trumpet to arms,
   Through the land let the sound of it flee,
Let the far and the near, all unite with a cheer,
   In defence of our *Liberty Tree*.

Democracy has indeed, like Paine's tree, both roots and fruits. It can be justified by either and is doubly justified by both. In waging a revolution, where all is precarious, one uses such means as are available to inspirit morale and to lessen the hazard. The roots of this tree are laid deep in a sense of inner dignity issuing therefrom as a self-respect so sturdy that it can respect other men also. That men all support some such sense of dignity is certain, and it is observable that upon it many build a sturdy self-respect. Everyone must have been impressed at times with the thought (and surprised at its utter impracticality) that, since some people are to one himself obviously no good, they would certainly admit it if one went to them and called their attention to the simple fact. Surprise, however, can only be the lot of one who acts upon this satisfying form of self-evidence, surprise and chagrin. No man will admit that he's no good, not at least to those who accuse him. Every nobody is a somebody to at least one body.

Building upon this most elemental of all facts, democracy assumes as the root of all justice this self-respect operating reciprocally. This is the bedrock meaning of what Paine has described as "the illuminating and divine principle of the equal rights of men."[20] Yes, the deepest meaning of the democratic dogma of equality is that pride is universally distributed among men. This very pride it is which constitutes the main prod to self-maintenance and to social progress. So arising easily from this bedrock fact is the postulate of eighteenth-century thought, that of the perfectibility of man. Such rootage is adequate to support the deep democratic faith in progress. This would be the psychological and sociological way of exposing the roots of democracy. While alive to this approach, Paine lived in an age as sophisticated in theology as it was simple in psychology and unsophisticated in anthropology. Living at such a time, it was natural if not inevitable for

[20] *Ibid.*, p. 130.

Paine to appropriate the argument from antiquity. This is an external approach to the roots of democracy. "The error," observes Paine, "of those who reason by precedents drawn from antiquity . . . . is that they do not go far enough into antiquity."[21] Appealing, then, from antiquity to antiquity more remote, Paine outbacks the backers-up until, in a golden age with God the creator, he backs conservatives off the map —or thinks to do so. In the proper antiquity, as he concludes, "Our enquiries find a resting-place and our reason finds a home."[22] By this direct appeal to the Maker of men, Paine thought to circumvent the bogus rights over men of those whom he regarded as pretenders to piety and of what he called "upstart governments, thrusting themselves between, and presumptuously working to *un-make* men."[23] All this was well enough as against presumptuous "unmakers" of men. But it raises, or at least raised, a question regarding the "maker" of men.

Men who can dispute about the rights of men can also dispute about the wrongs of God. By accepting the appeal to antiquity as the main approach to the roots of the tree of democracy, Paine found himself involved in an argument which no man, not even a revolutionary, ever wins—a theological argument. Not only did Paine not win his case; he all but lost his cause. Certainly he lost his popularity and his American influence for his and many another generation. Surprisingly so to him. Men who are too long on ideals are always skidding upon the habits of those more earthy. After his *Age of Reason*, written to prevent the French Revolution from sliding into godlessness, these stabler men of habit called Paine an infidel, called him a perpetrator of sacrilege, called him at last (Theodore Roosevelt) "a dirty little atheist."

Yet what Paine was trying to do in this theological approach to amelioration was to prevent the rights of men from

---

[21] *Ibid.*, p. 129.      [22] *Ibid.*, p. 130.      [23] *Ibid.*

being turned into wrongs against men by bogus claimants to
divine sanction operating hand in glove with perfidious governments. Paine wanted to show against the atheistical that
God exists and against the tyrannical that God is good. A
good God would have made man right and would have prescribed for him a prosperous pursuit of happiness. Paine did
not go so far as to venture with Ingersoll, Paine's successor in
nineteenth-century disfavor, that an honest god is the noblest
work of man; but he did believe fervently that God is at least
as good as man, even as good as a revolutionary; and in the
antiquity anterior to that of the conservatives a good God was
standing watch above his own. Against the revolutionary
spirit which insists that God is at least as good as the best
men, there always lingers in memory's background a fearful
picture of God as worse than the worst men. It was against
this fearful faith in *diabolus* as deity that Paine thought he was
struggling in his *Age of Reason*. If he could have foreseen the
inevitable penalty of his appeal to antiquity and to God—
roots primeval of his sacred "liberty tree"—he would have
been wise to emphasize exclusively, as of course he did mainly,
the fruits of that noble tree.

We ourselves shall now attend to the fruits, before contem-
plating through his eyes and ours the whole living tree of
democracy, rooted deeply and full of fruit in season. More
emphatically in Paine's century than in our own, but appropriately in any century, the fruits of democracy may be total-
ized as happiness. "Oh, Happiness," as Pope, the poetic voice
of Paine's century, exclaimed, "Oh, Happiness, our being's end
and aim!" Paine was fond of quoting Dragonetti to the same
effect in prose: "The science of the Politician consists in fixing
the true point of happiness and freedom. Those men would
deserve the gratitude of ages, who should discover a mode of
government that contained the greatest sum of individual

happiness, with the least national expense."[24] Indeed, Paine elevates to be the final criterion of government and the lasting goal of revolution this which Bentham was later to call the "felicific calculus." "If systems of government can be introduced less expensive and more productive of general happiness than those which have existed, all attempts to oppose their progress will in the end be fruitless."[25]

Democracy, then, has its roots and its fruits, and both Paine claims to be superior to anything existing. Its visible alternative, monarchy, has also its roots and fruits, rotten roots and rottener fruits. The pull of the ideal is matched by the push of the unideal, and all history is a hedonic adjustment of this push of pain and pull of pleasure. Let us now look at this larger perspective, appealing with Paine and his contemporaries to both antiquity and posterity. If antiquity has been democratically less popular as an appeal, it may be because democrats are disadvantaged by conservatives in any appeal to habit or custom. The past is man's worst enemy—it foredooms his future to be always less rosy than ideals can easily make it appear. We say that the past is dead; but the present is quick with the past, and the future is compromised by that quickness. We shall in the last chapter of this book be quoting the evolutionary Holmes to the effect that antiquity can be prudently neglected in the strategy of a wise life; the past will take care of itself in spite of all we may do to make the future different—"historical continuity with the past is not a duty, it is just a necessity."

Let us turn, therefore, with Paine's wiser turning—to posterity as democracy's best appeal. Carl Becker has beautifully shown how posterity functioned in eighteenth-century philosophy—functioned, in fact, as secular substitute for "the heavenly city" of earlier ages of sacred faith. Paine's use of pos-

---

[24] *Common Sense*, p. 37.    [25] *Rights of Man*, p. 152.

terity is well illustrated, though by no means exhausted, by the neat turn he makes against Colonial tories. They were appealing for peace in their time for the sake of their children. Paine counters:

As parents, we can have no joy in knowing that this government is not sufficiently lasting to ensure anything which we may bequeath to posterity: and by a plain method of argument, as we are running the next generation into debt, we ought to do the work of it, otherwise we use them meanly and pitifully. In order to discover the line of our duty rightly, we should take our children in our hand, and fix our station a few years farther into life; that eminence will present a prospect which a few present fears and prejudices conceal from our sight.[26]

And he concludes:

Wherefore, since nothing but blows will do, for God's sake let us come to a final separation, and not leave the next generation to be cutting throats under the violated unmeaning names of parent and child.[27]

With the future all things are possible, if the future be but extended indefinitely. It is the function of every revolutionist to extend the future far enough to give him opportunity to work his will upon habits always recalcitrant to present progress. Tomorrow is the brightest idea in any revolutionary lexicon.

Paine himself lived to see one of his revolutions, the American, measurably succeed; the other, the French, measurably fail. Each revolution in France, during his time, produced fruits so bad that it took another revolution to correct it. Jefferson, seeing the relative infertility of the revolutionary process, observed that through the Revolution with all its cost the French had succeeded in getting only about what they could have had from the king by concession, without any revolution at all. Paine, the apostle of perfection, was not himself too happy at the outcome of even the American Revolution. He

---

[26] *Common Sense*, p. 26.          [27] *Ibid.*, p. 29.

accused Washington of perfidy, of betraying the Revolution which Paine had helped to win.

But it was, whatever Paine thought, the presence of evolutionists like Washington and Hamilton and Jefferson which made the American Revolution the success it was, and it was the absence of such men that left the French Revolution to whatever failure it became. America had, and France had not, the Federalist papers. The betrayal of the Revolution is necessary to save the life of the revolution. That is a paradox which to understand will prepare us for and bring us to our latest American voice, that of Justice Oliver Wendell Holmes. It will also show us what of truth there is in Paine's deep conviction (4) that government though necessary is always evil.

### EQUIVOCAL GOOD, AND THE EVIL OF GOVERNMENT

The basic evil in government, we may remark as our third observation on Paine's philosophy of revolution, derives from the equivocal nature of the good itself, upon which the revolutionist fixes his single eye. Good must become flesh in order to dwell among us; it must get itself a human carrier, I mean, and must link its fate with his career. But when it reaches this level of incarnation, it is no longer unequivocally good. It meets its chief opposition in other good men, men who are the determined carriers of other meanings of the good. No sooner do such mortal carriers meet than their goods begin to mingle, not to say to tangle. From this tangle, only compromise can issue, which to every revolutionist is an evil. The only substitute for revolutionary action is action by agreement, and this involves not only accommodation of the concrete interests of men but also compromise of their consciences as well. This is what no whole-hearted revolutionist as such can stand. The presence of a sterner breed is required to save the revolution—not *from* betrayal, as the revolutionist conceives it, but, we may now correct, *through* betrayal, as the evolutionist conceives the process. As I have argued elsewhere,[28] this requires a type of personality which we know best in politicians, odious enough to the revolutionary, "the man with too many ideals."

Paine's friend, the other "iniquitous Tom," Thomas Jefferson, is a splendid example of such a type. An illustration from Jefferson's life will disclose the limit of Paine's philosophy without depreciating its necessity to revolution. On one particular occasion Jefferson was confronted with a choice which Paine, I suppose, could not have consummated without feeling that he had made "a whore of his soul." It was the choice of saving the revolution which Paine had helped to make. Jefferson elected to "betray" it. He himself minces no words about what he did, though some of his friends tried to persuade him not to tell the world so specifically in his autobiography what he had done. He gave in to Hamilton on a matter crucial and odious, the matter of the federal government's assuming the debts not only of the Confederation but of the states as well. He traded enough votes of his friends to Hamilton to put over the assumption and got in exchange the Capital permanently for Virginia. It was an odious compromise, which Jefferson malodorously describes:

. . . . the Assumption was passed, and twenty millions of stock divided among favored States, and thrown in as a pabulum to the stock-jobbing herd. This added to the number of votaries to the Treasury, and made its chief the master of every vote in the legislature, which might give to the government the direction suited to his political views. . . . . When this sop played its influence out, another engine of dominance must be contrived. . . . . This engine was the Bank of the United States. All that history is known, so I shall say nothing of it.[29]

[28] *The Legislative Way of Life* (Chicago: University of Chicago Press, 1940) and *The Promise of American Politics* (Chicago: University of Chicago Press, 1936).

[29] *Works,* "The Anas," IX, 95.

Let no omission or commission of emphasis obscure from us what Jefferson did. His action represents fairly the price somebody must always be paying for the preservation and perfection of democracy. It holds the secret of how democracy, established in revolution, can save itself only through evolution. Without dishonoring Paine and what revolution demands, it honors Justice Holmes and what evolution requires. It explains both the downright honor and the reputational dishonor of the politician in democratic societies. Note what Jefferson admits that he did: he not only arranged a compromise which his good friend White accepted with "a revulsion of the stomach almost convulsive," but he knowingly put into the hands of Hamilton the whole future fiscal policy of government by making the treasury of the United States the patronage trough, as Jefferson regarded it, whereby Hamilton could become "the master of every vote in the legislature which might give to the government the direction suited to his political views." One of the progeny of his compromise became the parent, as Jefferson saw, of that iniquitous child against which Jackson struggled, the Bank of the United States, and of that equally iniquitous grandchild against which Woodrow Wilson struggled, the monopolistic system arising from tariffs and other one-sided governmental favors. All this issues from Jefferson's own mouth to damn him and his breed forever as "low compromising fellows." Could Paine have made such a choice? Not likely. Could the Paines of our day or of any day do it? Hardly.

Why, then, did Jefferson do it? How, then, could Jefferson have done it? How can the Jeffersons of our day, or any day, do it? One cannot but admire the undramatic way in which Jefferson explains, with hardly a word turned edgewise to justify himself. "I thought it impossible," said he, "that reasonable men, consulting together coolly, could fail, by some mutual sacrifices of opinion, to form a compromise which was to save the Union." He does not further essay to justify himself. His action, if justifiable, is self-justifying. The Union, established by revolution, was worth saving, and worth what the saving of it would cost. This consideration it was which moved Lincoln throughout the Civil War to make compromise after compromise otherwise morally odious: to save the Union.

The moral cost of democracy is terrific—the cost of saving revolutionists from themselves and of preserving their product against their imprudence. It is a sacrifice of conscience in all matters save that which matters most—the achieving of the end for which revolutions are fought. It is a betrayal of the revolution from the point of view of the shortsighted, but not from that of the long-headed and the stout-hearted. To these latter it is the sacrifice of "personal opinions," as Jefferson had it, in order to save what is more than any opinion, the truth of the great ideals for which revolutions are fought.

Such are some of the inner sacrifices of peace which, no less than those of war, "try men's souls." It requires stamina to be thought crooked and corrupt by fellow-citizens, who admit that they are better than the politicians because they do not have to make the hard choices made by politicians. Those are the sacrifices which no dictators can make, or can allow their citizens to make—the sacrifices of admitting that, abstractly, one opinion is as good as another and that all must be adjudged compromisable about which honest men disagree. Such disagreements represent the inner tensions which democracy must stomach and resolve. The price includes and underscores the adult capacity to choose evils, many evils, but to choose in dark days the lesser evils with the same resoluteness that one chooses, in happier days, the greater goods.

Such considerations as these write small and poignant the price paid the world for the fact that government is itself an evil, but an evil necessary to civilization. They represent the final knowledge that good grows only in a composite soil made up of evil-and-good. But this is a story all its own, a story to which, after Professor Knight's brilliant delineation of it around liberty, we shall revert and which we shall embellish through the philosophy left preciously on deposit for the nation by that other American voice, the evolutionary voice of Justice Oliver Wendell Holmes.

### III. THOMAS PAINE: FLAMING SYMBOL OF HUMAN HOPE

The two attitudes toward democracy—the romantic and the realistic—we may here appropriately put together to body forth in form of beauty the democratic justification for both revolution and evolution. Nowhere is better formulated the inner meaning and the necessity of the two than in Shelley's ever living colloquy between the conservative (*First Spirit*) and the radical (*Second Spirit*), the radical having the last glorious word, as was appropriate for Shelley's own revolutionary bent.

### THE TWO SPIRITS: AN ALLEGORY

*First Spirit:*

> O thou, who plumed with strong desire
> > Wouldst float above the earth beware!
> A Shadow tracks thy flight of fire—
> > Night is coming!
> Bright are the regions of the air,
> > And among the winds and beams
> It were delight to wander there—
> > Night is coming.

*Second Spirit:*

> The deathless stars are bright above;
> > If I would cross the shade of night,
> Within my heart is the lamp of love,
> > And that is day!

And the moon will smile with gentle light
   On my golden plumes where'er they move,
The meteors will linger round my flight,
      And make night day.

*First Spirit:*

But if the whirlwinds of darkness waken
   Hail, and lightning, and stormy rain?
See, the bounds of the air are shaken—
      Night is coming!
The red swift clouds of the hurricane
   Yon declining sun have overtaken;
The clash of the hail sweeps over the plain—
      Night is coming!

*Second Spirit:*

I see the light, and I hear the sound.
   I'll sail on the flood of the tempest dark
With the calm within and the light around
      Which makes night day;
And thou, when the gloom is deep and stark,
   Look from thy dull earth, slumber-bound;
My moon-like flight thou then mayst mark
      On high, far away.

.   .   .   .   .   .   .   .   .   .   .   .   .

Some say there is a precipice
   Where one vast pine is frozen to ruin
O'er piles of snow and chasms of ice
      Mid Alpine mountains;
And that the languid storms pursuing
   That winged shape forever flies
Round those hoar branches, aye renewing
      Its aery fountains.
Some say when nights are dry and clear,
And the death-dews sleep on the morass,
Sweet whispers are heard by the traveller,
      Which make night day.

And a silver shape like his early love doth pass,
Upborne by her wild and glittering hair,
And, when he wakes on the fragrant grass,
He finds night day.

So we distant children of the Revolution of '76 find it—
"find night day"—at least in heroic prospect, though "the
death-dews sleep on the morass." As we patriotically find it
so, or resolutely struggle in war and peace to make it so, we
do well to mix a modicum of piety with out pride, and drop a
grateful thought, if not also in each anniversary season a rev-
erent tear, upon the long-neglected grave of Thomas Paine.
He too was gadfly to ever graceless tyranny. He was and is
the west wind of human hope, harbinger in darkness of our
democratic way.

# II

# THE RHETORIC OF THE DEBATE OVER THE ADOPTION OF THE CONSTITUTION

## CLARENCE H. FAUST

✿

WHEN the Federal Convention, which had under-taken to work out a new Constitution for the United States of America, finished its deliberations in September, 1787, the process of establishing a new government was but little more than well begun. There remained the difficult task of persuading the people of the country to adopt the new system. It was necessary for the proponents of the Constitution to convince their fellow-citizens that the proposed government would serve their varied interests, and that it conformed to the political principles they cherished. There were formidable objections to be met on every side. As state conventions were assembling to debate the question of ratification, the new Constitution was attacked and defended in pamphlets, newspaper essays, and editorials. Much of the work was anonymous, appearing over such signatures as "A Federal Farmer," "A Columbian Patriot," "A Citizen of America," "A Landholder," "A Plebeian," "Cato," "Caesar," "Cassius," "A Plain Dealer," and "A Steady and Open Republican."[1] The ablest and most permanently valuable contribu-

---

[1] See Paul Leicester Ford (ed.), *Pamphlets on the Constitution of the United States, Published during Its Discussion by the People, 1787–1788* (Brooklyn, 1888) and *Essays on the Constitution of the United States, Published during Its Discussion by the People 1787–1788* (Brooklyn, 1892).

tion to the controversy was a series of essays signed "Publius," the work of Hamilton, Madison, and Jay, which appeared in several New York journals, and were collected in book form under the title *The Federalist*.

These documents, and particularly *The Federalist*, have been studied and restudied to determine the causes which produced the American system of government; and the results of such study have, generation after generation, followed the changing fashions of historical research. In the 1850's George Curtis traced the history of the framing of the Constitution as a triumph of the "spirit of republican liberty" over the dangers of anarchy on the one hand and of monarchy on the other. Among the "facts that explain the circumstances under which the Convention was assembled, and which will enable us to appreciate the results at which it arrived"—and, indeed, first among these facts—according to Curtis, was the desire to frame a system of government "by which the forms and spirit of republican liberty could be preserved."[2] In 1882 George Bancroft found in the records of the debate over the Constitution support for his thesis that the establishment of the government of the United States was the culmination of a divinely guided process of moral improvement. Against "those who persuade themselves that there is in man nothing superior to himself," he wrote, "history interposes with evidence that tyranny and wrong lead inevitably to decay; that freedom and right, however hard may be the struggle, always prove resistless." Indeed, Bancroft began his discussion of the colonial system of the United States with the declaration that

[2] George Ticknor Curtis, *History of the Origin, Formation, and Adoption of the Constitution of the United States* (New York, 1865), II, 5. "The Constitution of the United States was the means by which republican liberty was saved from the consequences of impending anarchy. . . . . The alternatives, therefore, that presented themselves to the generation by whom the Constitution was established, were either to devise a system of republican government that would answer the great purposes of a lasting union, or to resort to something in the nature of monarchy" (*ibid.*, I, xi).

for a time wisdom and peace and justice dwelt among men, and the great ordinance, which could alone give continuance to the union, came in serenity and stillness. Every man that had a share in it seemed to be led by an invisible hand to do just what was wanted of him; all that was wrongfully undertaken fell to the ground to wither by the wayside; whatever was needed for the happy completion of the mighty work arrived opportunely, and just at the right moment moved into its place.[3]

Later historians read the records of the debate over ratification as support for the view that the Constitution of the United States was the product of the Teutonic genius for political democracy. American descendants of Teutonic invaders of England, according to this interpretation, inheriting the political ideals and talents of the race, had designed and set into operation the great democratic institutions of this country.[4] More recent writers have inclined to pitch their interpretations somewhat lower and to find evidence in the controversial literature concerning ratification of the decisive influence of economic interests in the framing and adoption of the new Constitution. "The Constitution," says Charles Beard, "was essentially an economic document," and the movement for it "was originated and carried through principally by four groups of personalty interests which had been adversely affected under the Articles of Confederation: money, public securities, manufactures, and trade and shipping."[5] Still more recently the debate over adoption has been interpreted by reference to the propensity of mankind to seek peace and security after periods of revolutionary agitation, the conflict over rati-

[3] George Bancroft, *History of the Formation of the Constitution of the United States of America* (New York, 1882), I, 5–6; II, 98. See also Bancroft's "The Necessity, the Reality, and the Promise of the Progress of the Human Race, 1854" in *Literary and Historical Miscellanies* (New York, 1855), pp. 481 ff.

[4] See Charles A. Beard, *An Economic Interpretation of the Constitution of the United States* (1939 ed.), pp. 2–3.

[5] *Ibid.*, p. 324.

fication being in this view the natural tension of revolutionary and "thermidorean" tendencies.[6]

These interpretations leave room for a somewhat less ambitious and sweeping consideration of the constitutional debate—an inquiry, not into the causes of the formation of such a Constitution, but into the devices for securing its adoption. Whatever value essays such as those written by the authors of *The Federalist* may have as signs of the historical forces—cosmic, racial, economic, or psychological—by reference to which the Constitution may be explained, their contemporary purpose was to persuade the people of the United States to ratify the work of the Federal Convention. They present, therefore, an interesting rhetorical problem. By what methods of persuasion did men like Hamilton and Madison—who, it has been observed, were as skilful in political debate as they were wise in political theory—undertake to convince their fellow-citizens of the desirability of the system of government proposed by the Constitutional Convention? By what kinds of argument did they hope to bring about a concert of opinion sufficiently widespread and sufficiently potent to put the proposed government into operation?

The problems that men like Hamilton and Madison faced as rhetoricians can best be understood by reference to their problems as statesmen during the deliberations of the Philadelphia Convention. The fundamental problem of the Constitutional Convention was to devise a political structure which would sufficiently conform to the different principles of government held by the delegates, and sufficiently satisfy the various interests they represented, to have a reasonable chance of adoption. It was not so much a problem of political education as of political adjustment—or, as Hamilton put it, of political "accommodation." Formulas had to be invented or dis-

---

[6] Samuel Eliot Morison and Henry Steele Commager, *The Growth of the American Republic* (New York, 1937), I, 162.

covered which would, on the one hand, conform to the political philosophies represented in the Convention and, on the other hand, offer the prospect of serving the divergent interests of the country.

In both of these aspects the task of the Convention was complex and difficult. Deeply rooted convictions concerning the principles of government had to be taken into account and a discouraging number of clashing interests had to be safeguarded if the new Constitution was to be made acceptable to the public and to have a fair prospect of success in practice. So directly opposed, for example, were the interests of the large and of the small states that the Convention was long and sharply divided between adherents to the Virginia, or large-state, plan and proponents of the New Jersey, or small-state, plan. The pressing question was not, as has been asserted, whether there was truly a natural conflict between the real interests of large and small states as such, but rather how the opposed opinions concerning these interests could be reconciled. Valid or invalid, the opinions of both parties had to be taken into account if a Constitution was to be devised which would insure the adherence of the necessary majority of American citizens. No less difficult was the task of reconciling what have recently been called "the real divisions of interest in the country"—divisions between North and South, between the commercial and agrarian parties, between the creditor and debtor classes. Each of these was itself split up into rival groups. Charles Pinckney, delegate from South Carolina, found it necessary, for example, to distinguish between

five distinct commercial interests. 1. the fisheries & W. India trade, which belonged to the N. England States. 2. the interest of N. York lay in a free trade. 3. Wheat & flour, the Staples of the two Middle States (N.J. & Penna.). 4. Tobo. the staple of Maryd. & Virginia & partly of N. Carolina. 5. Rice & Indigo, the staples of S. Carolina & Georgia.

Pinckney's inferences from this analysis may serve to suggest the difficulties the Convention faced in devising a system which would satisfy, not merely the general commercial interests of the country, but the representatives of rival commercial interests as well. Pinckney argued that the rivalry he had described would be "a source of oppressive regulations, if no check to a bare majority should be provided." The southern states, he said, were willing, as "a pure concession" to grant the new government the power of regulating commerce, but they would do so only if they were assured that commercial regulations would require the assent of two-thirds of the members of each house.[7]

"The natural situation of this country seems to divide its interests into different classes," Hamilton told the New York Convention in his argument for ratification. These gave rise to "delicate and difficult" contests. "It became necessary, therefore, to compromise, or the Convention must have dissolved without effecting any thing." There was, Hamilton insisted, nothing else to be done. "Any other system would have been impracticable. Let a convention be called to-morrow," he challenged his hearers. "Let them meet twenty times—nay, twenty thousand times,—they will have the same difficulties to encounter—the same clashing interests to reconcile."[8]

When the Convention was over, Washington felt obliged to conclude his letter of transmittal with the observation that

[7] Gaillard Hunt and James Brown Scott (eds.), *The Debates in the Federal Convention of 1787 which Framed the Constitution of the United States of America Reported by James Madison* (New York, 1920), p. 483.

[8] "Speech on the Compromises of the Constitution," in Henry Cabot Lodge (ed.), *The Works of Alexander Hamilton* (New York, 1903), II, 12–13. This view was acceptable to the ardently Anti-Federalist author of "The Letters of a Federal Farmer," who wrote, "the plan proposed is a plan of accommodation" and added that "it is in this way only, and by giving up a part of our opinions, that we can ever expect to obtain a government founded in freedom and compact" (Ford, *Pamphlets on the Constitution*, pp. 285–86).

the Constitution could hardly be expected to meet the full and entire approbation of every state. He could only hope that each state would consider "that had her interest alone been consulted, the consequences might have been particularly disagreeable or injurious to others." "The Constitution we now present," he said, "is the result of a spirit of amity, and of that mutual deference and concession which the peculiarity of our political situation rendered indispensable." And he concluded that it was "liable to as few exceptions as could reasonably have been expected."[9]

As moralists, some of the signers of the Constitution might deplore the preoccupation with sectional or private interests exhibited in the Convention. As economists, they might doubt the validity of some of the opinions concerning interests expressed and insisted upon by the delegates. But as statesmen it was their task to work out if possible a series of proposals which would satisfy the demands of the interest groups whose support was essential to the establishment of the new union. As good statesmen, they were obliged to go a step further. They were duty bound to make sure that the formulas agreed upon would in practice serve the interests they were designed to win over, lest the new government should prove impermanent because of the defection of those whose expectations had not been realized.

But the problems of the Convention were even more complex and troublesome than a survey of the interests to be reconciled might suggest. There were those who held as tenaciously to opinions concerning the proper principles of government as others held to opinions concerning the advantages, economic and social, which it ought to provide. To win anything like general consent, the Constitution had to be so framed as to conform to prevailing conceptions of what a government ought to be, as well as to hold out the prospect of

[9] Max Farrand (ed.), *Records of the Federal Convention* (New Haven, 1911), II, 665–66.

serving the important interest groups of the nation. To many Americans in 1787, for instance, no government could be acceptable which violated, or threatened to violate, the principle of state sovereignty. The government of the United States, they insisted, must be a federal government, rather than a national or consolidated one—that is, it must be set up by the states and operate through the states, rather than derive its authority from, and exercise it directly over, the individual citizen. It was on this ground that Patrick Henry attacked the new Constitution during the debate on adoption in the Virginia Assembly. With even more than his usual nervous eloquence, he challenged the right of the Philadelphia Convention to employ the phrase "*We, the people*" instead of "*We, the states.*" What was proposed, he warned the Virginia Convention, was not a confederacy of states, but a consolidated national government, based on principles "extremely pernicious, impolitic, and dangerous."[10]

There were those, too, who insisted that the national government should conform to what they called "revolutionary" or "republican" principles. The debate in the Convention over the resolution guaranteeing a republican constitution to each of the states indicates the divergence of opinion on this point. While Mason and Randolph declared a provision to secure republican government to be essential, Gouverneur Morris thought the resolution "very objectionable." "He should be very unwilling," he told the Convention, "that such laws as exist in R. Island should be guaranteid."[11]

It was, indeed, one of the commonest complaints concerning the Convention's work that in framing a new government insufficient attention had been paid to those principles for which, as it was put, a bloody revolution had just been

[10] Jonathan Elliot (ed.), *The Debates in the Several State Conventions on the Adoption of the Federal Constitution* (Washington, 1836), III, 22, 44.

[11] Hunt and Scott, *op. cit.*, p. 280.

fought. Were the new Constitution to be adopted, said Patrick
Henry, the change would be "as radical as that which separated us from Great Britain." As he saw it, the rights and
privileges won at great cost in the Revolution were in danger.
We "do not now admit the validity of maxims which we once
delighted in," he charged. "We have since adopted maxims of
a different, but more refined nature—new maxims, which tend
to the prostration of republicanism." The language of the
new Constitution was not, he said, the language of democracy.
"If, then, gentlemen, standing on this ground, are come to
that point, that they are willing to bind themselves and their
posterity to be oppressed, I am amazed and inexpressibly as-
tonished." The new government he found "incompatible
with the genius of republicanism." For its system of checks
and balances he had only contempt. "What can avail your
specious, imaginary balances, your rope-dancing, chain-rat-
tling, ridiculous ideal checks and contrivances?" "You are
not to inquire," he declared, "how your trade may be increased, nor how you are to become a great and powerful
people, but how your liberties can be secured."[12]

There were many who shared Patrick Henry's conviction
that it would be

considered a most extraordinary epic in the history of mankind that
in a few years there should be so essential a change in the minds of
men. It is really astonishing that the same people, who have just
emerged from a long and cruel war in defence of their liberty, should
now agree to fix an elective despotism upon themselves and their
posterity.

The author of the widely read "Letters of a Federal Farmer"
told his fellow-citizens that

there are certain rights which we have always held sacred in the
United States, and recognized in all our Constitutions, and which,
by the adoption of the new Constitution in its present form, will

[12] Elliot, *op. cit.*, III, 44, 50, 54, 137.

be left unsecured. . . . . Every man of reflection must see [he added] that the change now proposed, is a transfer of power from the many to the few, and the probability is, the artful and ever-active aristocracy, will prevent all peaceful measures for changes, unless when they shall discover some favorable moment to increase their own influence.[13]

And the Anti-Federalist governor of New York, George Clinton, urged the citizens of that state, in a letter published in the *New York Journal* over the signature of "Cato," to "compare your past opinions and sentiments with the present proposed establishment." "You will find," he declared, "if you adopt it, that it will lead you into a system which you heretofore reprobated as odious."[14]

Other Americans insisted that the new government must conform to the principle of absolute separation of legislative, executive, and judicial power; or that, to be satisfactory, it must not fail to include that essential element of a government formed by compact, namely, a detailed bill of rights.

Certain cherished principles of government, then, as well as certain jealously guarded interests, needed to be taken into account by those who hoped to frame a Constitution acceptable to the majority of their fellow-citizens. It seemed an all but impossible task. Charles Pinckney of South Carolina later wrote: "When the general convention met, no citizen of the United States could expect less from it than I did, so many jarring interests and prejudices to reconcile."[15] Small wonder that the Convention seemed, on more than one occasion, to be on the verge of dissolution, "scarce held together," as Luther Martin put it, "by the strength of an hair though the papers were announcing our extreme unanimity." Small wonder, too, that, when the Convention had completed

---

[13] "Letters of a Federal Farmer," in Ford, *Pamphlets on the Constitution*, pp. 311, 317.

[14] "Letters of Cato," in Ford, *Essays on the Constitution*, p. 263.

[15] "A Republican," in Ford, *Essays on the Constitution*, p. 412.

its work, no one seemed completely satisfied. Hamilton put the matter bluntly. "No man's ideas," he said, "are more remote from the plan than mine own are known to be." And, within a week after adjournment, Madison gave it as his opinion that "the plan, should it be adopted, will neither effectually answer its national object, nor prevent the local mischiefs which excite disgust against the state government."[16] With his usual political shrewdness, Franklin had argued in the closing days of the Convention for unanimous approval of the instrument that had been devised, not on the ground that it perfectly satisfied him (he confessed, indeed, that "there are several parts of this Constitution which I do not at present approve"), but on the ground that he doubted his infallibility and hoped that on this occasion others might have some little doubt concerning their own.

If every one of us, in returning to our Constituents, were to report the objections he has had to it, and endeavour to gain partisans in support of them, we might prevent its being generally received, and thereby lose all the salutary effects and great advantages resulting naturally in our favor among foreign Nations as well as among ourselves, from our real or apparent unanimity. Much of the strength and efficiency of any government in procuring and securing happiness to the people, depends on opinion, on the general opinion of the goodness of the Government, as well as of the wisdom and integrity of its Governors.

He moved, therefore, that the document should be signed under what he called a "convenient" and Madison described as an "ambiguous" form—namely, "Done in Convention by the unanimous consent of *the States* present," instead of by the consent of the delegates present.[17]

[16] Quoted by Edward P. Smith, "The Movement towards a Second Constitutional Convention in 1788," in J. Franklin Jameson (ed.), *Essays in the Constitutional History of the United States* (Boston and New York, 1889), pp. 49–50.

[17] Hunt and Scott, *op. cit.*, pp. 577–79.

As political philosophers men like Hamilton and Madison might reject some of the political principles strongly urged upon the Convention, but as statesmen they contented themselves, for the most part, with taking into account what they could not correct, hoping to devise proposals that would in some measure conserve the interests they had at heart and conform to principles they regarded as valid, and that would at the same time offer the prospect of satisfaction to those whose desires or conceptions of government differed in some respect from their own. The problem of the framers of the Constitution, to put the matter in another way, was to secure agreement, not on all subjects, but upon one fundamental matter— the structure of a new government. What was essential was general agreement upon the articles of a new Constitution. It was not essential that all who approved that Constitution should do so with exactly the same ends in view. Otherwise the task would, from the first, have been hopeless. Nor was it essential that the approval of the instrument should rest on precise agreement concerning the principles of government. That was likewise hopeless. Interest groups with widely separated ends and political philosophers with various conceptions of the nature of government might co-operate successfully, however, in framing a Constitution if, for one reason or another, they could agree upon the desirability of establishing a particular machinery of government.

I do not mean to suggest that the Convention, by envisaging its function as the achievement of agreement concerning the particular structure of government, thereby assumed a simple and easy task. Agreement concerning the details of governmental machinery was possible, as the event proved— though, as the event likewise proved, it was difficult and laborious. Though ends could to some extent be left general and diversified, and though precise formulation of principles could in part at least be waived, it was still essential to specify in detail the parts and mode of operation of the new government. The character of the legislative body or bodies, the methods of election to them, and the nature of powers assigned; the methods for appointing judges, their tenure, the precise authority of the courts—all these matters had to be precisely specified. And on each of them general agreement had of necessity to be secured.

When the Convention had finished its arduous undertaking, and all but a few of its members had signed the document which their labors had produced, there remained the difficult task of persuading the country that the work had been well done. Supporters of the Convention's proposals had to persuade the state conventions to ratify them against the protests of a determined, energetic, and skilful opposition.

Neither party, it must be confessed, was overnice in its selection of weapons. No small part of the argument revolved, indeed, not around the merits and demerits of the proposed plan of government, but around the merits and demerits of the proposers and their opponents. Charges of wilful wickedness and inexcusable stupidity were cast back and forth. Oliver Ellsworth of Connecticut, writing over the signature "A Landholder" in a series of widely circulated newspaper essays, dismissed the opponents of the Constitution as including but three classes. First, there were those, according to "A Landholder," who opposed a federal government because they were "old friends of Great Britain, who in their hearts cursed the prosperity of your arms" and have ever since delighted in the perplexity of your councils—men whose "hopes of a reunion with Great Britain have been high," and who expect that the defeat of the measure now proposed will accomplish their end. A second, and no more respectable group, consisted of "debtors in desperate circumstances, who have not resolution to be either honest or industrious. . . . . Paper money and tender acts, is the only atmosphere in which they

can breath, and live." The third, and apparently in the Landholder's view the most dangerous and despicable class, consisted of "men of much self importance and supposed skill in
politics, who are not of sufficient consequence to obtain public
employment, but can spread jealousies in the little districts of
the country where they are placed."[18]

The Landholder's charges were favorite topics of Federalist
argument. Every person "who either enjoys, or expects to enjoy, a place of profit under the present establishment," wrote
"A Friend of the Constitution" (probably Daniel Carroll) in
the *Maryland Journal*, "will object to the proposed innova-
tions, not, in truth, because it is injurious to the liberties of his
country; but because it affects his schemes of wealth and consequence."[19]

Even Benjamin Franklin turned his hand to the delineation
of the character of Anti-Federalists. In an article entitled "A
Comparison of the Conduct of the Ancient Jews and of the
Anti-Federalists in the United States of America" he undertook to show that Anti-Federalists had such an aversion for
good government that, like their biblical prototypes, they
would have rejected a constitution framed by the Deity himself and supernaturally communicated to them. Like the ancient Hebrews, he said, they retained an affection for the land
of their nativity, or a passionate attachment to the golden
calf, or a distrust of their leaders, sufficient to blind their eyes
to the excellence of the new government and to turn their
hearts from it.[20]

It is not to be imagined, of course, that Anti-Federalists
endured without remonstrance the reiteration of charges of
this kind. Nor, indeed, were they content simply to assume

[18] "A Landholder," in Ford, *Essays on the Constitution*, pp. 143–44.

[19] *Ibid.*, p. 335.

[20] Albert Henry Smyth (ed.), *The Writings of Benjamin Franklin* (New York, 1907),
IX, 698.

the defensive. They replied in kind. Charged with desiring
to maintain influence in petty local spheres of politics, they
countered with the accusation that Federalists were greedy
for tyrannical authority. The plan, they asserted, had been
designed to bring power and wealth to its framers. The author of the "Letters of Agrippa," which appeared in the *Massachusetts Gazette*, declared that if we were "to judge of what
passes in the hearts of federalists when they urge us, as they
continually do, *to be like other nations*, and when they assign
mercenary motives to the opposers of their plan, we should
conclude very fairly they themselves wish to be provided for
at the publick expense. . . . . Power and high life are their
idols, and national funds are necessary to support them."[21]
Elbridge Gerry, who had been a member of the Philadelphia
Convention on appointment from Massachusetts, and who had
refused to sign the Constitution, wrote even more bitterly in
1788 of the "deep-laid plots, the secret intrigues, or the bold
effrontery of those interested and avaricious adventurers for
place, who intoxicated with the ideas of distinction and pre-
ferment have prostrated every worthy principle beneath the
shrine of ambition."[22]

[21] In Ford, *Essays on the Constitution*, p. 89.

[22] "Observations," in Ford, *Pamphlets on the Constitution*, p. 5. The author of these
observations was himself involved, and that as chief figure, in one of the bitterest of
the controversies over personalities in the literature of the debate concerning ratification. His refusal to sign the document which the Constitutional Convention had drawn
up gave him a prominence which the Federalists could not well overlook. A few weeks
after the Convention Oliver Ellsworth addressed an open letter "to the Honorable
Elbridge Gerry, Esq.," in which he explained, on the authority of a member of the
Convention, that Gerry's refusal to sign the Constitution was simply the result of
"rage and resentment" because the Convention had rejected his proposals concerning
the redemption of the Continental currency, of which he was a large holder. Gerry
replied, in no tenderer tone, and Luther Martin of Maryland came to Gerry's defense
in a series of letters written for the *Maryland Journal* which concluded with the judgment that "falsehoods of the kind promulgated by the Landholder, so groundless, so
base and malignant, could only have originated or been devised by a heart which would
dishonor the midnight assassin." This pronouncement did not, of course, conclude the
controversy, which came thereafter simply to involve both Luther Martin and Gerry in
a bitter quarrel. Ford, *Essays on the Constitution*, pp. 127–33, 172–74, 341–52.

The authors of *The Federalist* turned on occasion to arguments of this kind, though they managed to state them with an air of impartiality and a dignity of phrase which lifted their work above that of bitterer and pettier contemporaries.[23] But, for the most part, Hamilton, Madison, and Jay concerned themselves with the problem of winning adherence to their cause by persuading their readers that the proposed government promised them many advantages and that it conformed to the political principles cherished in America. They preferred to specify at length the ways in which the new national government would serve the various interests of the country, and to stress the aspects in which it conformed to certain prevailing political doctrines.

They began by considering in great detail "the utility of union," urging the adoption of the new government as a protection against foreign dangers, as a safeguard against dissension between the states, and as a restraint on domestic factions. Turning thereafter to more positive advantages, they argued for the efficacy of the union in encouraging commerce, in securing revenue, and in accomplishing economy in government. They followed their arguments on these points with an almost equally elaborate analysis of the insufficiency and impotence of the existing Articles of Confederation for the purposes of good government. And then, having established the desirability of the proposed union as a means to achieve a series of important ends, they undertook, in the famous thirty-ninth essay, to prove its conformity, in certain essential respects, to republican principles.

In establishing these two points—the utility of the union and its republican character—the authors of *The Federalist* had recourse to two kinds of arguments. Their proof of the advantages of the new Constitution in producing peace, tranquillity, and prosperity for the country rested upon premises concerning causes and effects—general maxims, for the most part,

[23] See Nos. 1 and 24, for example (Random House edition).

about the causes of peace and war, of domestic tranquillity and disturbance, of commercial success or failure, together with propositions concerning these matters, drawn from the experiences of earlier political societies. The Federalist arguments concerning the conformity of the proposed system to republican ideals were, on the other hand, developed largely by definition. To establish the "conformity of the plan to republican principles," Madison framed, for example, a careful definition of the term "republic" and then carefully matched his definition with the proposed Constitution. He defined a republic as "a government which derives all its powers directly or indirectly from the great body of people, and is administered by persons holding their offices during pleasure, for a limited period, or during good behavior." And he followed the definition with a demonstration that the proposed government was "in the most rigid sense, conformable to it."[24]

The authors of *The Federalist* were not content, however, to pursue independent lines of argument in an effort to win the approval both of those chiefly concerned with the advantages to be derived from the new national government and of those who needed reassurance concerning the rightness of its principles. Going a step further, they undertook to prove, on the one hand, the utility of republican principles and, on the other hand, the conformity to cherished political principles of the means designed to secure national peace and prosperity. For this purpose they traced out the desirable results of adopting republican principles and offered evidence for defining as republican the governmental machinery proposed to serve the nation's interests. They attempted, it might be said, to prove that what was right was also useful, and that what was useful was also right. Thus it is the point of one of the best known of the essays—the tenth, on the safeguards promised by the

[24] No. 39. See in this connection Hamilton's "Brief of Argument on the Constitution of the United States," which begins with an elaborate examination of the meaning of the word "republic" (Lodge, *op. cit.*, II, 91 ff.).

new government against the dangers of faction—that the best
protection against factional convulsions is a government
framed in accordance with republican principles. In such a
government power is delegated to a small number of citizens,
elected by the rest, so that public views may be refined and enlarged by passing them through the medium of a chosen
body "whose wisdom may best discern the true interests of
their country and whose patriotism and love of justice will be
least likely to sacrifice it to temporary or partial consideration." Since these advantages are more certain when the
territory encompassed by a republic is large and contains factions determined in many ways, a republican union of the sort
proposed would afford the best possible protection against
factional disturbances:

Among the numerous advantages promised by a well-constructed
Union, none deserves to be more accurately developed than its tendency to break and control the violence of faction. The friend of popular governments never finds himself so much alarmed for their character and fate, as when he contemplates their propensity to this
dangerous vice. He will not fail, therefore, to set a due value on
any plan which, without violating the principles to which he is
attached, provides a proper cure for it.

In short, what was defined and cherished as right in principle
was upon a careful calculation of causes and effects discovered
to be in fact useful. It was, furthermore, seen not merely as
protection against factions, but as a safeguard for republican
principles.

We thus behold [Madison wrote] a republican remedy for the dis-
eases most incident to republican government and according to the
degree of pleasure and pride we feel in being republicans, ought to
be our zeal in cherishing the spirit of supporting the character of
Federalists.

The authors of *The Federalist* found good reason, furthermore, for reversing this relation on occasion, so as to show
not merely that what was known to be right could also be

shown to be useful but that what was for other reasons desirable or useful could also be shown to be proper and right. Thus it is the purpose of the thirty-ninth essay to prove that the kind of government which the needs of the country had been shown in earlier essays to demand is "strictly republican" in principle. No other form of government, Madison wrote, "would be reconcilable with the genius of the people of America; with the fundamental principles of the Revolution; or with that honorable determination which animates every votary of freedom, to rest all our political experiments on the capacity of mankind for self-government." If, then, the proposals of the Convention deviate from these principles, no matter how effectively the new government may serve the interests of the country, "its advocates must abandon it as no longer defensible." Having premised this much, Madison proceeded to define the term "republican" and then to prove that "on comparing the Constitution planned by the Convention with the standard here fixed, we perceive at once that it is in the most rigid sense conformable to it."

It was, in short, the strategy of *The Federalist* to make clear that both consideration of interests and concern with principle, entertained separately or variously related, compelled support for the new Constitution. They argued that its conformity to certain cherished ideals of government would have the happy result of serving certain important interests of the country; and they insisted that, among the important ends it might be expected to achieve, not the least important was the safeguarding of certain ideal political forms. Thus, to put the matter somewhat loosely, the political idealist and the citizen preoccupied with his own private interests were both to be satisfied, not merely by being shown different elements of the proposed scheme, but by being led to see the ideal excellence of its practical provisions and the practical advantages of its ideal form.

The success of Federalists in their endeavors to exhibit both the practical advantages and the political orthodoxy of their proposals is indirectly attested by the complaint of one of their sharpest opponents, the author of the "Letters of a Federal Farmer," that "the radical defects in the proposed system are not so soon discovered" because, on the one hand, of "the democratic language" used in formulating it, and because, on the other hand, the "temptations" presented

to each state, and to many classes of men to adopt it are very visible. . . . . The eastern states will receive advantages so far as the regulation of trade, by a bare majority, is committed to it: Connecticut and New Jersey will receive their share of a general impost: the middle states will receive the advantages surrounding the seat of government: the southern states will receive protection, and have their negroes represented in the legislature, and large back countries will soon have a majority in it. This system promises a large field of employment to military gentlemen, and gentlemen of the law; and in case the government shall be executed without convulsions, it will afford security to creditors, to the clergy, salary-men and others depending on money payments.[25]

The success of the complex appeal of Federalists to interests and to principles is indirectly revealed, furthermore, in the way in which historians have discovered support in the statements of the Federalists for such widely different explanations of the movement for a new constitution as those proposed by Curtis and by Beard. The documents which convinced Curtis that the "great object" of the framers of the new system of government was to preserve "the forms and spirit of republican liberty" reveal to Beard that the system was the product of "a group of economic interests which must have expected beneficial results from its adoption."[26]

In appealing to those who were primarily interested in the

[25] "Letters of a Federal Farmer," in Ford, *Pamphlets on the Constitution*, p. 319.
[26] Curtis, *op. cit.*, II, 5, and I, 417-18; Beard, *op. cit.*, pp. 17 and 152 ff.

benefits government might provide, and who were therefore concerned with means and ends rather than with conformity to abstract principles, the authors of *The Federalist* faced a difficult problem. The interests to be satisfied were many and, if not always in open opposition, at least not invariably harmonious. Commercial interests must be encouraged to expect much of the new Constitution, while agricultural interests must not be alarmed at the prospect of encouragement to commerce. Men primarily interested in the protection of property must be assured that the new government would serve them well, while others concerned with the preservation of individual freedom must not be frightened by the prospect of severe regulation in favor of property. The great landholding and commercial interests of the country must be enlisted without giving further support to the often repeated charge that the government had been designed by, and was to be administered in favor of, the rich and the well-born.

What the authors of *The Federalist* did was to trace out a complex series of advantages for each of the important provisions of the Constitution so as to make it clear that various interests would be served at one and the same time. It was in this way, for example, that they dealt with the provision allowing the national government to maintain a standing army in times of peace. There had been great opposition to this provision in the Philadelphia Convention; and the attacks on it, as constituting a danger to the rights of states and of individuals, were frequent in Anti-Federalist pamphlets and essays. Gerry of Massachusetts had argued in the Convention that it was a mistake to provide no check against standing peacetime armies. The people, he said, would be "jealous on this head, and great opposition to the plan would spring from such an omission." He insisted, consequently, that the national peacetime army should be limited to two or three thousand. The motion had been supported by Luther Martin, but it had been decisively rejected by the Convention.[27]

Several of *The Federalist* essays were, therefore, devoted to a defense of the Constitution on this point. In an early paper Hamilton dismissed the contention that standing armies constituted a danger to liberty by insisting that it rested upon a mistaken analogy between our situation and that of Great Britain, where a standing army might furnish the king with the means for imposing tyrannical rule.[28] When somewhat later Madison came to consider systematically the powers vested in the new government, his argument for giving the federal government an indefinite power of raising troops both in time of peace as well as in time of war was more complex. A national standing army, he said, was not only necessary to protect the nation against foreign aggression but would actually serve as a safeguard of its liberty. Without a union protected and supported by military force, America not only would be at the mercy of her enemies but must eventually be divided into small states, each maintaining, as well as being maintained by, a standing army. "Nothing short of a Constitution, fully adequate to the national defense and the preservation of the union," he argued, "can save America from as many standing armies as it may be split into States or Confederacies, and from such a progressive augmentation of these establishments in each as will render them burdensome to the properties and ominous to the liberties of the people, as any establishment that can become necessary, under a united and efficient government, must be tolerable to the former and safe to the latter." A national standing army is necessary, in short, for the preservation of union; and union is, in turn, necessary for the protection of property and the preservation of liberty against the dangers of military establishments in the states. Madison does not leave this appeal to a variety of interests in defense

[27] Hunt and Scott, *op. cit.*, p. 424.          [28] No. 8.

of the constitutional provision for a standing army merely to inference. "This picture of the consequences of disunion," he wrote, "cannot be too highly colored, or too often exhibited. Every man," he added, "who loves peace, every man who loves his country, every man who loves liberty, ought to have it ever before his eyes, that he may cherish in his heart a new attachment to the union of America, and be able to set a due value on the means of preserving it."[29]

In much the same way, Hamilton's analysis of the commercial utility of the new union is extended to embrace its advantages for preserving the political institutions cherished in this country and for preserving the national honor. Europe, he argued, is naturally unfriendly to our prosperity, and that in a variety of ways. She would like to monopolize "the profits of our trade" and to clip "the wings by which we might soar to a dangerous greatness." Were we to be disunited, Europe might fix the price of our commodities and snatch from us the profits of our trade. As a means to these oppressive commercial measures, she would attempt "to prescribe the conditions of our political existence"; and the extension of her dominion must be accompanied by humiliation for America.

The superiority she has long maintained has tempted her to plume herself as the Mistress of the World, and to consider the rest of mankind as created for her benefit. Men admired as profound philosophers have, in direct terms, attributed to her inhabitants a physical superiority, and have gravely asserted that all animals, and with them the human species, degenerate in America—that even dogs cease to bark after having breathed awhile in our atmosphere. Facts have too long supported these arrogant pretensions of the Europeans. It belongs to us to vindicate the honor of the human race and to teach that assuming brother moderation. Union will enable us to do it. Disunion will add another victim to his triumphs. Let Americans disdain to be the instruments of European greatness! Let

[29] Nos. 23–29, 41.

the thirteen States, bound together in a strict and indissoluble union, concur in erecting one great American system, superior to the control of all transatlantic force or influence, and able to dictate the terms of the connection between the old and the new world!

Thus Hamilton, not content merely to enlist at this point those only whose interests were limited to trade, enlarged his discussion of the commercial advantages Americans would enjoy under the new Constitution to show that these benefits were connected with their honor and even that of mankind.[30]

Among the devices by which the authors of *The Federalist* undertook to appeal both to a wide variety of interests and to cherished principles of government, none is more important than the way in which they elevated the conflict of interests to a principle of good government. They not only took pains to furnish assurances that interests of various sorts would be adequately served, and to make clear how particular provisions of the Constitution could be expected to serve several distinct interests at the same time, but they insisted that the public good and private right could best be guarded by a governmental system that provided for the expression and interplay of numerous and divergent interests. One of the chief ways, according to *The Federalist*, whereby factional disturbances will be controlled in so extensive a republic as that proposed for the United States of America is by the great "variety of parties and interests" in the new nation, so that it will be "less probable that a majority of the whole will have a common motive to invade the rights of other citizens; or if such a common motive exists, it will be more difficult for all who feel it to discover their strength, and to act in unison with each other."

The influence of factious leaders may kindle a flame within their particular States, but it will be unable to spread a general conflagration through the other States. A religious sect may degenerate into

[30] No. 11.

a political faction in a part of the Confederacy; but the variety of sects dispersed over the entire face of it must secure the national councils against any danger from that source. A rage for paper money, for an abolition of debts, for an equal division of property, or for any other improper or wicked project, will be less apt to pervade the whole body of the Union than a particular member of it; in the same proportion as such a malady is more likely to taint a particular county or district, than an entire State."[31]

This line of argument in *The Federalist* does not depend upon the assumption that selfish interests will be held in check by disinterested majority opinion. The argument is rather that in a properly constructed government the public good emerges out of a conflict of interests. As Madison put it:

This policy of supplying, by opposite and rival interests, the defect of better motives, might be traced through the whole system of human affairs, private as well as public. We see it particularly displayed in all the subordinate distributions of power, where the constant aim is to divide and arrange the several offices in such a manner as that each may be a check on the other—that the private interest of every individual may be a sentinel over the public rights.[32]

I am not interested at the moment in the soundness or unsoundness of this theory, nor in determining the extent to which it may be taken as a fundamental conviction of the Federalists, but rather in the rhetorical advantages it presented to Federalist writers. The proposed government, they argued, might be expected to preserve the numerous and diverse interests of the country. They took pains, also, to make clear that in many respects at least these interests were not in conflict—that the provision for a standing army, for example, would help to satisfy the desires of those primarily concerned about peace, or the national honor, or the preservation of a republican form of government, as well as the desires of those primarily concerned with the protection of property.

[31] No. 10.                    [32] No. 51.

But they went a step beyond this to reassure the members of interest groups that the foresight of the Constitutional Convention had provided for their safety by devising a governmental system in which the various conflicts of interest would serve in a measure to safeguard the rights and interests of each. "It is of great importance in a republic," they said, "not only to guard the society against the oppressions of its rulers, but to guard one part of the society against the injustice of the other part. Different interests necessarily exist in different classes of citizens. If a majority be united by a common interest, the rights of the minority will be insecure." The best method, they continued, of providing against this evil is to comprehend "in the society so many separate descriptions of citizens as will render an unjust combination of a majority of the whole very improbable, if not impractical." In the federal republic of the United States "the society itself will be broken into so many parts, interests and classes of citizens, that the rights of individuals, or of the minority, will be in little danger from interested combinations of the majority. In a free government the security of civil rights must be the same as that for religious rights. It consists in the one case in the multiplicity of interests, and in the other in the multiplicity of sects."[33]

This careful attention of the Federalists to the variety of interests represented in the country, as well as to the political principles cherished by its citizens, was, of course, subordinate to their concern with the various specific provisions of the new Constitution. They might appeal to a variety of interests in urging the advantages of the new government, and might recognize various political principles in justifying it; but they were obliged by the nature of their problem to secure agreement concerning the structure of the proposed government. General agreement concerning ends and principles was

[33] *Ibid.*

not essential to their purpose, but difference of opinion concerning the parts and structure of the government would defeat the hopes of ratification. It was necessary, consequently,
that the authors of *The Federalist* should persuade their readers to approve in detail the proposed arrangement of the
branches of government, the proposed modes of selecting public servants, and the proposed assignments of governmental
authority.

It was not necessary that these provisions should be regarded as perfect, but it was essential that they should be viewed
as good. Hamilton and Madison were ready, therefore, to
grant that the Constitution was imperfect, insisting only that
it was as good as could reasonably be expected, and far better
than the Articles of Confederation under which the nation
had been governed. For this purpose, they postponed the detailed consideration of the house, the senate, the executive,
and the judiciary until such consideration had been prepared
for by a general discussion of the advantages and of the theoretical soundness of an energetic national government having
the character of a federated republic. To these general considerations, and to the general necessity of the powers of military
defense and of taxation assigned to the government, they
devoted roughly half of the eighty essays which constitute
*The Federalist;* and then, before plunging into the discussion
of the various powers conferred by the Constitution and the
precise structure of the proposed government, they discussed
at some length "The Difficulties of the Convention in Devising
a Proper Form of Government." The purpose of this discussion was to lighten their burden of proof concerning the
details of the new government by offering good reasons for
not expecting perfection in the Constitution. "Many allow-
ances ought to be made," they pointed out, "for the difficulties inherent in the very nature of the undertaking referred
to the Convention."

Their statement of the first of these difficulties served the double purpose of making their immediate point and of strengthening an important part of their case for the Constitution. It was that the existing Articles of Confederation had been so imprudently and unsoundly devised as to offer the Convention no worthy precedent to follow. Thus, even in granting the imperfections of the Convention's work, Madison managed to suggest the complete inadequacy of the only other system of government available to the American people.

Madison's statement of the second difficulty of the Convention—"that of combining the requisite stability and energy of government with the inviolable attention due to liberty and to the republican form"—involved a shrewd recognition of the rhetorical problem of convincing the American people that the government would serve their interests adequately and would at the same time conform to prevailing political principles. The authors of *The Federalist* had done their best, as we have seen, to avoid the sharp opposition of these two considerations. Madison here minimized the importance of any lack of success in this undertaking by confronting his readers with the difficulty of reconciling principles with interests, while at the same time he prepared for objections that might be raised to the details of the Constitution on this ground.

Another serious problem which had rendered the task of the Convention arduous, according to Madison, was that "of marking the proper line of partition between the authority of the general and that of the state governments." On this point Madison shrewdly uncovered a threefold difficulty, the analysis of which armed him amply with topics for dealing in detail with the provision of the Constitution. One element of the great difficulty of the Convention's task, he pointed out, was the complexity of the affairs with which the Convention had to deal. This difficulty, he added, was greatly increased by the imperfections of the human mind, which rendered men's conceptions concerning these affairs inaccurate. And it was further increased by the inadequacies of language. The objects of thought, he pointed out, are in their very nature complicated. The processes of thought are lamentably inaccurate. And the devices for its expression are unfortunately ambiguous.

Besides the obscurity arising from the complexity of objects, and the imperfection of the human faculties, the medium through which the conceptions of men are conveyed to each other adds a fresh embarrassment. The use of words is to express ideas. Perspicuity, therefore, requires not only that the ideas should be distinctly formed, but that they should be expressed by words distinctly and exclusively appropriate to them. But no language is so copious as to supply words and phrases for every complex idea, or so correct as not to include many equivocally denoting different ideas. Hence it must happen that however accurately objects may be discriminated in themselves, and however accurately the discrimination may be considered, the definition of them may be rendered inaccurate by the inaccuracy of the terms in which it is delivered. And this unavoidable inaccuracy must be greater or less according to the complexity and novelty of the objects defined. When the Almighty himself condescends to address mankind in their own language, his meaning, luminous as it must be, is rendered dim and doubtful by the cloudy medium through which it is communicated.

Here, then, are three sources of vague and incorrect definitions: indistinctness of the object, imperfection of the organ of conception, inadequateness of the vehicle of ideas. Any one of these must produce a certain degree of obscurity. The Convention, in delineating the boundaries between the federal and State jurisdictions, must have experienced the full effect of them all.[34]

The expectations of the readers of *The Federalist* were not, in short, to be pitched too high as they approached the critical discussion of the Convention's proposals concerning the

[34] No. 37.

precise structure and powers of the government. Madison had prepared the way for pointing out later, in the discussion of article after article of the Constitution, the great complexity of the problems addressed, the difficulty of forming clear conceptions of them and of conceiving clearly their solution, and the inadequacy of language for stating the Convention's proposals exactly. He had in a measure prepared his readers to agree with him in the conclusion that "the real wonder is that so many difficulties should have been surmounted, and surmounted with a unanimity almost as unprecedented as it must have been unexpected."[35]

The difficulties which the Federal Convention met and conquered in framing the new Constitution were not much more formidable than those which Federalists faced and overcame in persuading the country to adopt the Convention proposals. These difficulties were, furthermore, of the same kind: the problem of the framers of the Constitution had been to reach agreement among themselves, despite the differences in their interests and ideals, concerning an elaborate system of proposals for a new government; the problem of Federalist writers was to secure the general consent necessary for the establishment of the proposed machinery of government by enlisting the support of the divergent interests of a country already complex in its concerns and by obtaining the sanction of the cherished political principles of its headstrong inhabitants. Their methods of winning popular support for the Constitution were of essentially the same kind as the methods by which the members of the Convention had managed to reach agreement among themselves.

A fuller and more precise examination of these methods— the methods by which American democracy solved its problems in what has, not without reason, been called "the critical period of American history"—might be expected to be of

[35] *Ibid.*

some instruction to this generation, which finds itself in another critical period of our history. The authors of *The Federalist* were themselves convinced that their problems were of far more than merely local or immediate importance. In the first number of *The Federalist* Hamilton wrote:

It has been frequently remarked that it seems to have been reserved to the people of this country, by their conduct and example, to decide the important question, whether societies of men are really capable or not of establishing good government from reflection and choice, or whether they are forever destined to depend for their political constitutions on accident and force.

The question Hamilton presented to Americans has in our day assumed world proportions. If after the present world convulsions we hope to establish an international organization "from reflection and choice," it may be wise for us to re-examine the work of the men who contrived an instrument for achieving coherence and co-operation among what threatened to be thirteen jealous sovereignties, and who found the means for persuading their fellow-citizens to ratify the plan they had worked out. It seems at this moment unlikely that the nations now at war will suddenly discover a single common interest on the cessation of hostilities, or unanimously embrace a single set of political principles. We shall wait long indeed if we wait for either of these things to happen. Our immediate hope may well rest upon statesmen wise enough to discover formulas for international co-operation that, without depending upon absolute agreement concerning the ends of government or concerning its ideal character, will lift the societies of men above dependence on "accident and force."

# III

# THE MEANING OF FREEDOM

## FRANK H. KNIGHT

✻

OUR task of defining freedom is itself to be interpreted in relation to the subject of our next chapter, to which this one is introductory. That is, freedom is to be defined as a social ideal, and considered from the point of view of its realization by appropriate social action. The aim of this chapter will be to survey the ambiguity and confusion which affect the concept of freedom in political and philosophical discourse and which consequently stand in the way of intelligent discussion of social policies aimed at progressive realization of the ideal.

It follows that we shall not be concerned with various meanings of "free" and "freedom" in general usage, where there is no fairly direct connection with our central problem. Examples are the use of the word "free" as a synonym for "gratuitous" or "costless," and as a synonym for "pure"— i.e., free from admixture or contamination, in a wide variety of connections, including morals. Even in the field of political discourse, freedom has become, in the context of modern culture, an "honorific" word (in Veblen's term), and one far more often used to arouse emotion, and to beg a question, than to communicate any objective meaning, of denotation or connotation. One need only think of "the land of the free and the home of the brave," or "When Freedom from her mountain height, Unfurled her standard to the air, . . . ." and similar poetry and rhetoric in the literature of other modern nations. In this chapter we shall discuss the meaning only of internal political freedom, without reference to the particular situation of not being ruled by foreigners.

Before taking up the problem of human and social freedom, however, we must call attention to the use of the term in physical science, and also colloquially, in connection with the behavior of inert objects; for this usage sheds an important light on our special problem. The physicist or engineer speaks as a matter of course of "free" motion, "free" flow, etc., and of degrees of such freedom. In everyday usage, also, the situation of an object released from the hand, or of a stone or an icicle released by natural causes from its point of attachment, would be described by saying that it is "free" to fall. Moreover, if we think of a falling object encountering an obstacle on its way to the ground, it would surely be correct to say that it is not "free" to fall farther. But we should hardly use this language of an object lying upon the ground! The difference clearly has to do with the notion of a "normal" position of rest and stability. We shall come back to this notion in connection with human freedom.

In relation to human beings and their conduct, we shall have to consider freedom at the three major levels or categories of intelligible discourse: as a fact, as a desideratum, and as an ideal or a value which is in some sense objective—i.e., as valued in a higher sense than "merely" being desired by someone. This third meaning of freedom, a right in contrast with a wish, is the most important for our subject, but it seems to be relatively modern. Discussion of freedom as a fact—i.e., the metaphysical problem of freedom—is surely much older, and the notion of freedom as a desideratum, in a particular sense, is perhaps the oldest of all. Since long before history, men have known what it meant to be bound or imprisoned or enslaved, and have considered this condition undesirable in comparison with freedom as its opposite. This is the common meaning of the term, for example, in the standard version of the English Bible, especially the Old Testament. In earlier times, such unfreedom was recognized as a great misfortune and aroused sympathy, even pity, but freedom was not classed as a "right" nor was slavery regarded as "wrong."

In the New Testament, we encounter the term in several varieties and shades of meaning within a quite different field. For example: "Ye shall know the truth and the truth shall make you free" (John 4:32); and "who shall deliver [i.e., free] me from the body of this death?" (Rom. 7:24). Such "mystical" conceptions of freedom are important for understanding the complex which men of today also crave or idealize as freedom. From the beginning of serious reflection about the issues of life, a craving for release or liberation from life as such, or from actual or possible earthly human life, became a conspicuous note in recorded utterances. It is especially characteristic of Hindu thought, both Brahmin and Buddhist, where it found expression in the Nirvana ideal. But a similar idea and craving are familiar in Greek and Roman literature, in early and later Christian mysticism, and even in modern English authors. One thinks of Shakespeare's Hamlet, in the familiar soliloquy, and in the description of the world as a goodly prison, "in which there are many confines, wards, and dungeons, of which Denmark's one o' the worst." Also the lines of Swinburne:

> From too much love of living
> From hope and care set free. . . . .

And Tennyson, the poet of evolution and progress, also wrote "The Lotus Eaters"; and even Browning, the romanticist and poet of action and struggle par excellence, says on one occasion:

> There remaineth a rest for the people of God
> And I have had trouble enough for one.

Other variations of what is ultimately the same theme are the
fascination with magic, supernatural or unlimited power, so
conspicuous in the Faust story as well as in the *Arabian Nights*,
and the praise of intoxication—literal, as in Omar, or figura-
tive, as in the lines from our own Walt Whitman,

> One hour to madness and joy. . . . .
> O, to drink deeper of the deliria than any other man!

To all these ideals, however (but most especially to quietism), is antithetically opposed the modern view of life, and
the concept of freedom which goes with it.  In contrast with
the religious-mystical yearning for freedom from freedom,
from life itself, we moderns view life as action, adventure, and
achievement, and our moral idealism centers in responsible behavior.  Yet something akin to the other note is prominent in
the current attitude of uncritical elevation of "security" to the
position of a supreme desideratum and social ideal.  We cannot
here stop to treat in detail the characteristic modern view of
life, with its fascinating combination and compromise between romanticism and rationality, but it must always be remembered that in his more profoundly reflective moods modern man may also incline to regard as a higher rationality the
"escape" from rationality ("me this unchartered freedom
tires"—and "Tintern Abbey," also by Wordsworth).  Moreover, some compromise between achievement and appreciation and between action and repose is necessary if one is to
live at all, whichever extreme is philosophically embraced.
It is literally impossible to be completely rational in either of
the antithetical meanings, the contemplative or the practical,
the mystical or the romantic.  We cannot think entirely without acting, even in parasitic monasticism, nor can we act entirely without thinking—or "think with our blood."  It is
an interesting fact that those who have held and advocated
the "escapist" ideal have had doubts about effective methods,

particularly about the effectiveness of suicide (as with Shakespeare's Hamlet) or about natural death as a solution.

Turning to our main problem, the meaning of human freedom in modern thought, it is appropriate to proceed from the simple to the complex, hence to begin with the notion of freedom in purely individual conduct, apart from social relations. For the purpose of analysis, it is necessary to employ the hypothesis of a "Crusoe," a device long since recognized as indispensable in economic theory. (We shall find later that economic freedom is the most important aspect of our practical problem.) The Crusoe hypothesis enables us to separate the three meanings of freedom already mentioned, freedom as a fact, as a desideratum, and as an ideal.

Let us suppose that our Crusoe, in wandering about his island, accidentally becomes entangled in jungle growth, or falls into an unobserved pit. Usage certainly justifies describing his situation as one of being "unfree," and his subsequent behavior as an effort to "free" himself. But if the situation is intensified, if Crusoe encounters a smooth perpendicular cliff upward or downward from his path, we should hardly think of him as unfree to proceed farther in that direction, but rather as simply "unable" to do so. The notion of individual unfreedom is clearly related to that of the unfreedom to fall of an inert object lying, say, upon a table, particularly in the abnormality of the situation, previously pointed out. Yet it is very different in that it presupposes the possession by the human being, Crusoe, of *desires* or interests, of some limited *power* to act, which is under his volitional control, and of "will," the power or capacity of choice. We may consider these three factors, beginning with the second, power (or "ability"), where the main source of confusion lies, as just suggested.

We do not think of a Crusoe as unfree to pass an obstacle when he knows beyond doubt that he does not control the power to do so, and consequently would not make the attempt, or even will the act. Moreover, if we modify the hypothesis by assuming that our man is completely disabled by the accident, we should again say that he has become unable rather than unfree to proceed. The problem of defining freedom is found to be that of clarifying the relationship between the desire to act and the power to act, in some desired way and against some obstacle or resistance. An ordinary person would not say that he or another is unfree to do anything which he "obviously" has not the power to do. We do not think of men as being unfree to lift mountains, or to fly (in the absence of suitable mechanical equipment), or to perform any feat calling for natural or acquired capacity or skill which they do not possess, nor do we think of a paralytic or a hopeless cripple as being unfree to engage in an athletic contest. Freedom, in its primary common-sense meaning, refers negatively to the absence of some more or less abnormal interference with acting in some normal way in which the individual would otherwise be able, would possess the power, to act.

A philosophical difficulty at once calls for notice here, in the relation between freedom and power (for an individual in a purely physical environment). It appears self-contradictory to say that a person has power and is not free to use it. Unfreedom must be due to the presence of some obstacle which he really does not have the power to overcome. The idea clearly is that he normally would be able to act but for some special obstacle; and it seems to be further implied that the relation between the obstacle or resistance and the power is in some way problematic or uncertain. Even if the situation is abnormal, with respect either to the resistance or to the "incapacitation" of the subject, we hardly describe him as unfree, or consider it rational for him to feel unfree, if the action is unquestionably impossible. If an individual wishes to perform an act which he thinks is within his power, and attempts it and fails, while he might feel unfree, an impartial observer to whom the impossibility was patent would undoubtedly disagree.

The freedom-and-power relation in action is also clearly relative to the wish to act. It would be nonsensical to say that a person is not free to do anything which he does not have, and under no realistically imaginable conditions would have, any desire to do, and it would be irrational for the person himself to feel unfree. Real freedom is rather increased by barriers to harmful or dangerous acts, such as the practice of having fences along the edge of ravines. In short, it seems that logically speaking an individual is free to do anything he both has power to do and wishes to do, and is not free to do anything else. We shall return to this point later.

I shall pass very briefly over the venerable question of the fact of freedom in the sense of the reality of choice, the metaphysical problem of the freedom of the will. This question is certainly answered in the affirmative by the very act of raising it as a question, or that of answering it either negatively or affirmatively. Machines do not raise the question with respect to themselves, and "we" do not raise or argue it with them. To deny freedom is to deny the reality of denying and to assert that error itself, as well as all effort, is an error, an illusion, and illusion itself an illusion. Beyond this, self-contradiction cannot go. It is literally impossible to assert that one is not asserting, or that there is no difference between making a statement and making a noise. Freedom is an ultimate datum of experience and a condition prerequisite to all discourse, even to all thinking.

Certain aspects of individual freedom of choice call, however, for further brief analysis. The ultimate fact of freedom is freedom of thought, the power or capacity to control one's own mental content—or not to control it. The deepest meaning of freedom is the power of choosing between choosing and

not choosing, the fact that the rational self-conscious being
"can" or is free to "set his fancy free." The meaning of the
word "free" in this phrase should be noted. The free, or
freed, fancy presumably follows some kind of natural or positive causality, analogous to the behavior of an inert object
falling "freely" under the force of gravity. Yet the subject re-
tains more or less continuously the power to "resume control." Again, choice, when it is made, may be either "arbitrary" or "rational," within some limits, but is always finally
arbitrary. One must finally stop the deliberative process at
some point and make an absolute decision on an intuitive
basis. The alternative is to go on thinking forever, and "that
way madness lies." Too much thinking is as bad as too little,
even none at all. One must decide where to stop. Furthermore, in choosing to choose, one must select somehow, among
an infinite number of questions which might be raised, subjects in connection with any one of which it would be possible
to exercise control over thinking.

When one has chosen to choose, to control his thinking, he
directs the activity in terms of "norms" of either an intellectual or an aesthetic character. He either solves problems or
chooses between different idea patterns (and/or feeling patterns) on the basis of some kind of immediate appeal or distaste, which is of the nature of beauty and ugliness. The
question whether individual choice necessarily involves objective "norms" beyond a personal preference need not be
argued here. It is relatively more difficult to avoid imputing
this normative quality to intellectual than to aesthetic judgments, harder to reduce truth to individual opinion than to
think of preference in other matters as based on "pure" taste,
without any question of "good" taste.

The second main aspect of freedom is freedom of overt action, a similar ultimate inscrutable power of choice over the
translation of thinking into action, where the thinking itself

involves some kind of imagined overt activity of the person. This is the psychological fact or activity of "innervation." Overt action, of course, begins with movements of the subject's "body," but an act includes any causal sequence of change in the external world which is intentionally initiated by bodily movements. It is, of course, in this field that all practical problems lie. Our problem of freedom lies in the narrower field of social action, including communication, which involves relations with other subjects; such individual choices and their consequences are to be interpreted in terms very different from those of the mechanical sequence of events in physical nature, but these must be considered first.

It may be said—it is commonly said, and seems admissible to say—that, in choosing some mode of overt action, one is ultimately choosing between patterns of future subjective experience, with some manipulation of the body and the external world as intermediary in such control. This seems to be contrary to the immediate facts of experience itself, a rationalization of the actual procedure. Rather, one chooses between courses of outside events. That is, the ultimate premise of choice in action (in a purely physical environment) is an intellectual or aesthetic interest in the external world. However, in considering the grounds of choice, we must take account of subjective factors, beginning with bodily pain and pleasure. Pain and pleasure are, in fact, inseparable from intellectual and aesthetic experience—with the exception, perhaps, of the cruder forms of pain (and, more doubtfully, a few very crude pleasures)—and this is one of the most important results of any realistic analysis of motivation. In connection with social relations, which in reality are always involved to an important degree in human choice (the Crusoe hypothesis being fundamentally unrealistic, though necessary for analysis), we encounter serious complications, and the grounds of preference consequently become vastly more difficult to describe or classify.

This analysis eliminates any valid and distinctive notion of freedom as a desideratum, for the isolated individual. Apart from social relations, freedom reduces to power to act (perhaps plus will power) in relation to desire and to the obstacle or resistance to be overcome in achieving any desired objective. Metaphysically, a solitary subject is as "free" in one situation as in another. He is always free to choose, in thought and action, between the "possible" alternatives; possibility is a matter of power, and power is what freedom as a desideratum really means. It is to be remembered that one has more or less control over one's desires, and in particular has some ability to choose desires which are more rather than less in harmony with one's power of action. It seems to be admissible to call attainable desires "rational," in comparison with those which are not attainable, as already observed. By carrying this principle far enough, and suppressing desire more or less completely, one may approach the ultimate freedom— freedom from freedom, annihilation, or mystical rapture, considered in our introductory section.

We should note that the rationality of having realizable rather than unrealizable desires is a very different matter from that of cultivating "better" desires. As a matter of fact, the consequences are rather in the opposite direction; for, in spite of the common romantic assumption to the contrary, the "higher" tastes are far more expensive than the lower. It seems reasonable to assume that a purely individualistic individual, such as we have taken our Crusoe to be, would not make critical judgments of any kind about his ends, but would deliberate and choose only in connection with the procedures for satisfying given desires. However we may think about a Crusoe, an unrealistic hypothesis at best, this is the assumption necessary for analysis—namely, that apart from social interests and influences the individual would choose in action entirely in terms of actual preferences, of "mere" taste, in contrast with any form of "good" taste, or an interest in truth. To say the same thing in other words, all choices, as conscious and rational, would be economic choices; the isolated individual is an "economic man," or a pragmatist; all of his thinking is instrumental, about means and their use in achieving given or found ends, not about the high or low quality of ends. In chapter iv we shall be much concerned with freedom in economic activity, and its relation to ethical ideals, but we need not here go into more detail with regard to its meaning.

By way of approach to the problem of the meaning of freedom in society it will be analytically useful to consider briefly another hypothetical situation, a modification of the Crusoe idea, and quite as unrealistic. Let us suppose, briefly, that instead of a single Crusoe there have all along been two shipwrecked men on the same island, but unaware of one another's existence, and that one suddenly discovers the other's presence in some accidental way. Leaving realistic details to your imagination (the hopes and fears aroused by a footprint in the sand!), and disregarding the innumerable interesting questions raised, let us further assume, in order to minimize the factor of interindividual relationships as a first step to our real problem, that both men—we might call them Crusoe and Drusoe, or simply C. and D.—are misanthropic, or lovers of solitude, and wish to continue their previous type of life. It is impossible. Their worlds will be utterly changed.

Even in this rather fanciful situation, C. and D. will confront the condition or high probability of conflicting interests, and must make arrangements of a new kind. It will be necessary for them to arrive in some way at an agreement delimiting their domains and spheres of interest. The alternative would be conflict, to the extent of an effort at mutual extermination. In the nature of men as purposive beings, it is strictly impossible for one human being to regard another as a mere fact in his own environment, to be dealt with in the same way as any other given condition. It is impossible even for one to subdue the other, and use him strictly as an instrument for his own purposes, without some "social" relationships of a very different sort. Such a purely instrumental attitude and relationship is, in fact, impossible for one of a pair, even if the other should consent to it and "co-operate" to the utmost extent of any human capacity to do so. Apart from the fact that conflict itself is a social relationship, and one which it is reasonable to assume is especially abhorrent to an antisocial individual, no permanent relationship is even theoretically possible, for two individuals living in the same "world," without some agreement, explicitly or tacitly accepted by both parties, delimiting spheres of action where interests do or may conflict. The agreement must be accepted as right—altogether or within the limits worth fighting for, a judgment in which power relations play a large role. And the judgment of rightness is arrived at by thinking which is very different in kind from the instrumental or economic thinking of the hypothetical isolated individual.

Thus at the ultimate minimum, if any two persons are to live in the same world—each being a recognized fact in the environment of the other—they must agree by rational ethical discussion on a body of "law." The alternative is that one must exterminate the other, to avoid being exterminated by him, or must establish some impenetrable boundary, of distance or in some other form, so that the two no longer inhabit the same world. In other words, any two persons confronted with the problem of "living together" in any manner or degree must establish a society (or accept one in which they find themselves). And, even in our ultra-simplified hypothetical situation of two shipwrecked men, the society established will be found to involve in principle all that is essential to any human society. The essence of society is a body of rules defining a boundary between spheres of action of its members and preventing violent or destructive clash in consequence of conflicting interests. Addition of any or all details of the largest and most complicated social order—("economic") co-operation, sociability, cultural intercourse, political machinery for making and enforcing the law, or any that may be thought of —does not change the essential principle. Men who live in the same world cannot be "free" in the sense in which a Crusoe is free. They become subject to a new and categorically different type of limitation or restriction on their activities, and freedom in society must be defined in entirely different terms. The task of the remainder of this chapter—in fact, the main task of the chapter as a whole, to which all that has gone before may be regarded as introductory—is to explore this field of meaning, to indicate in outline the content of the notion of freedom in society, which in turn defines the problem of organized social action.

The essential fact about human society, in consequence of which it presents social problems to its members, individually and as a group, is that human beings have both conflicting and common interests. In the absence of common interests (at a minimum the common interest of living in proximity) they would not associate at all; and in the absence of conflicting interests association would present no problems. This, of course, assumes as a prior fact that human beings have interests, which they strive to realize through action directed by thinking. If they were automata there would, of course, be no problems of any kind. Human life contrasts in this respect with that of animals, or with hypothetical animals, whose behavior is assumed to be instinctive, which is assumed to mean that it is mechanical. Such creatures might live either individual or social lives, and we recognize an approximation to the ideal of mechanistic social life in the elaborate organization found among the colonial insects, such as the ants and termites. We assume that they have neither individual nor social interests.

The essential category, the substance, of human society is law. But it is law in a distinctive meaning of the term, in which in turn the meaning and conditions of social freedom are to be sought. All life exemplifies law, as does also the behavior of inanimate things. The "activities," or more accurately the course of events, in a termite colony, in so far as this is really based upon instinct and in so far as instinct is really mechanical, are based upon law in the same meaning as inanimate behavior. To elucidate the nature of human society and its distinctive type of law, it is necessary to return for a moment to the hypothesis of a rational individual living in isolation, and to consider the meaning of law in relation to freedom in that connection.

The great bulk of the conduct of a free human being is unquestionably in accord with law in a meaning which must be described as ultimately physical or mechanical. Without going into detailed analysis, it is a mixture of instinct and habit, both of which are automatic types of response. The freedom of the individual is "marginal," and in fact quite narrowly limited. To some extent various "situations" in which an individual finds himself raise questions which call for deliberation and choice, and to some extent he has the mysterious power to raise questions even in situations in which his established behavior patterns (instinct plus habit) "might "automatically go into action. The range of freedom of choice is partly a matter of choosing in given situations, *ad hoc*, but far more largely a matter of reflectively modifying established patterns of response, or changing his "character." This is accomplished chiefly through deliberation and "self-legislation" carried on in the "calm cool hour," rather than in situations presenting immediate problems calling for solution, where there is little time for thinking.

With reference to human social life, we have first to stress the unreality of the hypothesis used above of previously isolated individuals coming together and establishing a society, a body of law, by "contract" in the literal interpretation. It should be obvious that, even more than in the case of an isolated individual, the conduct of individuals in social relations must be based upon "established" patterns; *ad hoc* decisions are infinitely more difficult. And in the great bulk of social behavior these established patterns have become habitual, and even unconscious. Presumably, again, they involve an ultimate core of instinct, but this has certainly receded in importance as the social unit has become larger and more complex and as the action patterns themselves have taken on more of the "artificial" character of civilization or culture. This is necessarily the case as society becomes more progressive or "dynamic." Relatively little is known about the evolutionary development of culture, and it is not in place here to attempt to go at any length into that problem. The socially inherited habits or established ways of doing of men in civilized society are referred to in their social aspect by the distinctive names of "customs" or "institutions." Presumably their original development was partly a phenomenon of unconscious and automatic processes, through an indefinitely long initial stage, and partly a product of conflict and domination, such as seems to prevail in the herd life of gregarious animals. In any case, human society is distinguished from animal societies, of either the insect-colony or the gregarious type, first of all by the phenomenon of cultural inheritance in contrast with biologically inherited instincts; and custom remains the primary meaning of law in human society. Lan-

guage is the basic law. Custom is still ultimately mechanical.
But man as we know him, who is always highly "civilized"
in comparison with any known animals, is characterized not
merely by the fact of custom, but by a strong disposition
against passive conformity, reflecting individual and conflicting interests; and human society is characterized by deliberate, organized control.

Law in its distinctive meaning in human society has gradually approached a form which may be called "contractual,"
as men have come to be conscious of their customs, to accept
them, to enforce them upon recalcitrant individuals, and
finally—much later, after an intervening stage of authoritarian
organization—to change them deliberately by conscious social
action. A society which has evolved to the point where it
makes its laws by inclusive group deliberation is a "free" society, or a "democracy." The infinite variety of structures
and procedures by which any group directly or indirectly
makes or formulates its laws, including public and constitutional law, and by which, at need, it enforces them, need not
be considered here. Our concern is with the twofold concept
of freedom under law and free law-making, or (internal) political freedom. In the ideal or perfect democracy there would,
of course, be no literal enforcement of law. The ideal is anarchy. It would mean complete agreement by "rational"
process (ethical, not economic, rationality) on all the concrete content of the law. Short of that, the members of a society may still agree on "fair" procedures for making the law,
and may voluntarily and rationally accept the results, even
while holding divergent opinions as to the rightness or ideal
character of the law as made, so that there is still no need for
coercion. This second ideal is approximated in modern de-
mocracies; literal enforcement through punishment (as a
threat) is restricted to a small "criminal" or incompetent element in the adult population, and to "infants." There is, of

course, no clear line between conformity to custom through mere suggestion and habit, conformity for rationally ethical reasons of either sort described, informal quasi-enforcement by social sanctions, and literally coercive enforcement by punitive procedure. This complex mixture of categories, none of which can be clearly defined, makes the problem of defining freedom, for practical purposes, an extremely difficult one.

The primary meaning of freedom in society is twofold—individual freedom in one's own defined sphere and "free association" in contrast with coercion. It is always a negative concept (the absence of coercion), and coercion is the term which must really be defined. Freedom as absence of coercion is freedom not to associate, either without consultation or on any terms openly offered, together with freedom to offer terms of association to others. Or freedom may be viewed positively as voluntary agreement on the terms of association, but it must be "rational" agreement and the terms must be "right." Persuasion is clearly a form of coercion—it is the use of a kind of force to control the action of another by controlling his thought. Coercion itself, it is to be noted, is a negative idea, consisting of prevention or deprivation. One being does not coerce another directly, but only by closing some alternative of action which would otherwise be open, or by threatening to do so, or by depriving or threatening to deprive the coerced subject of some benefit which he would otherwise enjoy.

The elementary meaning and function of law, as we have seen, is to prevent coercion, or clash, by drawing boundaries, defining spheres of action within which individuals are literally free, in the sense in which a Crusoe is free when he is the only individual in his "world." Law increases freedom when it is negatively coercive, preventing coercion and conflict. The ultimate limit of social freedom is realized when all the members of any social aggregate, who would otherwise infringe upon one another's spheres of individually free action, and so come into conflict, "freely" agree in the formulation of such boundaries. The boundaries still exist, and have essentially the same meaning, when individuals associate with any degree of intimacy in any way or for any purpose. In short, coercion arises or exists whenever one person associates with another or affects him in any way, and the terms of the relationship are not "voluntarily" and rationally accepted by the latter. Within a sphere of action defined by right law (in either of the meanings already distinguished), an individual is free in the purely individualistic or Crusoe sense. He is free to perform any acts which do not affect others at all, or affect them only in a way which they do not feel to be an infringement upon their own individualistic freedom—and which he wants to do and has the power to do. The individual himself is taken as given, as he stands, with respect to his desires and his endowment with power to act.

However, two important qualifications must be made for life in society, viewed as a "going concern." The first is that promises freely made must be kept; they must limit the freedom of the promisor in the future according to their tenor. The second qualification is similar but more sweeping. In social life, the established patterns of behavior involving relations between individuals come to involve a kind of quasi-contract or legitimate expectation, so that action by one party affecting the freedom of another includes any change in the pattern of action, even a mere failure to act in the expected way. It is this principle which gives rise in large measure to the empirical and practical problems of a free society, particularly where individual relationships have become widespread yet intimate and complex, as in the modern economic order. The typical individual tends to feel, and hence to believe, that he has a right to make nearly any change in his own course of action and that any restriction is an infringement on his freedom; but at the same time he claims the right, as a part of his own freedom, to have his own conditions of action exempt from injurious disturbance through changes by others in their routine. The contradiction is obvious; this combination of claims is virtually on a level with demanding the right to eat one's cake and still have it. It sets the main problem of our next chapter.

It follows from what has been said that freedom vs. coercion in social relations is an ethical concept and an ethical problem. In ordinary usage, indeed, freedom covers all ethics; it reduces to the notion of right and wrong, of justice and injustice, where in the case of a Crusoe it reduces to the notion of power. Coercion is any act or failure to act which "wrongs" another. The philosophical problem of defining freedom and coercion becomes that of defining right and wrong, in a society made up of given individuals, meaning "real" right and wrong, specifically in contrast with individual judgments and feelings. The latter are the primary data for the social psychologist and for "that insidious and crafty animal vulgarly called a statesman or politician" (in the words of Adam Smith). The task for the remainder of our inquiry is to point out two main facts about the problem of social right and wrong. First, we shall briefly contrast the notion of freedom and coercion, or right and wrong, under the assumption stated above that the individual is taken as given, with the problem raised by dropping this assumption, and inquiring into its validity. That is, we must consider the "rights" of an individual as he is in relation to his "right" to "be what he is," to have the power and the desires which he may actually have. (The right to act in terms of given desires and power involves the right to change both; the right to be what one is carries with it the right to become what one wishes to become, to the extent of one's "ability" to do so.) The second remaining problem, or topic, covers certain matters of expediency, where the practical exigencies of workaday social life set limits to freedom and other personal rights and make compromise necessary—and in that sense right.

A little attention to the assumption involved in taking the individual as given will reveal at once that, in comparison with actual usage, our definition of freedom as the absence of coercion, or even of wrongful coercion, is only a partial one. The term "freedom" as regularly used in political controversy covers a much wider scope than merely the absence of coercion. It is used, and in the highest of high places, as we shall point out, to refer even to the vague right of the individual to "freedom from" want and fear, a right to support and protection, without reference to possibilities or conditions. Even with this layer of spurious meaning "peeled off," as it were, and discarded, the term is still excessively broad and ambiguous. The conception of unfreedom is applied to a position of disadvantage or limitations upon an individual's range of action due to the absence of power to act, to his "poverty" in means of action, apart from interference by any other agent, whether rightful or wrong. It has become common in discussions of freedom to draw a distinction between these two conceptions, under the designation of negative and positive freedom. In fact, usage typically refers to the former in contemptuous terms as "merely" negative freedom, implying that real freedom requires possession of power to act. This is certainly a wasteful and confusing use of language. The word "freedom" ought to be restricted to some definite meaning and not used as a general designation for an ideal society—to say nothing of implying that every individual is unconditionally entitled to anything he seriously wants and to protection from anything he regards as a serious evil (both at the hands of democratic government), as is done in Mr. Roosevelt's "Four Freedoms."

Unquestionably, the sphere of activity open to an individual depends just as much on his endowment with power, means, or capacity (always relative to some resistance to be overcome in acting or enjoying as he would like to do) as it does on the absence of interference (or, more generally, of resistance to action). While it may seem futile to quarrel about usage, and the more so where usage is backed up by a strong prejudice, such as the urge to capitalize upon the emotional meaning of a word, it is difficult to see how reasonably accurate communication is possible unless such independent variables as freedom and power are kept separate by different names. As a minimum departure from usage it may at least be suggested that such terms as "formal freedom" and "effective freedom" would be less question begging and misleading than "positive" and "negative" freedom. Unquestionably, again, the individual's right to a rightful share in the distribution of means of action in society—whatever that may include, and where a reasonable possibility of social action exists as a basis for the social obligation—is a real ethical right. And the problem of having "society," however bounded, so organized and conducted, and having individuals so act, that all its members will come into adult life as individuals with a maximum proper endowment of the power to act which makes freedom effective in general and civilization possible is fully as important as the problem of formal freedom. In our next chapter we shall find that the central problem of economic life centers in these facts as to power, which in popular thinking are grossly misconceived in vital respects.

This brings us again to the fact that freedom, in the formal meaning of noninterference, takes for granted as a datum individual will, desire, or taste as well as power or means. This twofold assumption as to the given individual has always pervaded our traditional, "British-American" social philosophy of utilitarianism, which is weak, not to say fallacious, in this respect. But the current "neo-liberal" reaction against this view, in the direction of statism as a remedy for inequality, is political romanticism and even more dangerous. It must also be emphasized that the "rights of man," by whatever name they may be called, must include a rightful share in the entire cultural inheritance from the past. The right to the possession and free use of power must be conditioned by a corresponding assumption of responsibility on the part of the individual, who must have a cultivated outlook on life in general, "right" wants and tastes, knowledge of what are the worthwhile things, the true goods of life; and he must also know and recognize the limited possibilities of their realization.

To ignore this condition would mean, on the one hand, that society may be wrecked and civilization destroyed through insistence on impossible standards of equality; while, on the other hand, ignoring right wants as a condition necessary to freedom would mean that the slave—of another individual, of some group, or of the state (which would then consist exclusively of a superior caste)—would be as free as anyone, provided only that he were effectively "conditioned" to accept his lot and be satisfied with it. That this latter notion is by no means fantastic will be clear if we merely recall that in all culture prior to modern Western civilization the conception of freedom embodied in both secular and religious-ethical thought has accepted and justified slavery and other caste, class, or status differences. Even the author of our Declaration of Independence was a slaveholder, and a large proportion of those who fought for freedom in the Revolutionary armies regarded slavery as necessary and as divinely ordained. In recognizing as beyond question the necessity of both freedom and power, absolute and relative, to the good life, our modern world view inverts the axioms of our inherited religious-ethical tradition. The latter has always repudiated wealth, and all forms of power and capacity, practical intelligence, and taste, as obstacles rather than instruments to moral value, which it also verbally identifies with freedom. If this modern view of life is wrong, then all the main objectives which are set up or taken for granted in current social discussion and the struggle for betterment should be re-inverted; the general objective of social action would be to set the clock back to the medievalism of the Dark Ages, or to some kindred type of primitive life.

But the point here is that, in the long view, the social problem is not so much freedom—liberation—as it is the creation of individuals fit for membership in a free society. Civilized life requires that "man" wield power over nature, and progress rests on the growth of this power. But ethical idealism requires that individual men do not have final or irresponsible power over other individuals. Free society is largely a matter of the diffusion of the power which is necessary to effective freedom; and this diffusion, or fundamental equality, is dependent also upon a generalized disposition on the part of individuals to use power "rightly." In the short view, the social task of individuals is to live their lives within a framework of institutions; but, looking ahead, institutions must both be maintained and improved in the light of the type of citizen they will produce. Neglect of this long view of the problem may be charged to both our traditional religious (Judeo-Christian) ethics and to utilitarian liberalism. Both tended to treat ethics as a problem of right relations between given individuals, though utilitarianism emphasized freedom and progress, and power in the sense of productive capacity as a prerequisite, while the religious ethic ignored these factors, and even condemned efforts directed to their achievement.

On our last subtopic, which has been referred to under the head of "expediency," what needs saying is closely related to what has just been said in relation to the place of institutions in the social-ethical problem. Anyone who has studied history or reflected about the problems of life must be impressed by two facts. The first is that, in the long view, which is primarily the standpoint of social policy, society is a complex of institutions in a sense even more fundamental than that in which it is an organization of individuals and relationships between individuals. And the second fact is that institutions are highly resistant to change, and likely to be destructively disorganized by any effort to change them sweepingly or rapidly. Order, and an order which is generally understood, and even taken for granted, is after all the first requisite of civilized life and is also a primary condition for its improvement. This means that stability and gradualness, or conservatism in the true meaning of the word, must be the first objective in efforts directed to maintaining and improving the quality of life on the whole. Social institutions are embodied in customs and laws, which must be relatively stable in order to enable the individual to form expectations and to act intelligently, hence freely, in the significant meaning of the word, in relation to his social environment.

It is clearly a natural craving, deeply imbedded in human nature, and especially characteristic of "superior" individuals, to yearn to be "free" from the institutional order in which one finds one's self at a given time and place in history. The craving may, of course, take either of two forms—mere negative destructionism, or an urge to radical reconstruction. One thinks of the quatrain in Fitzgerald's *Omar* about grasping "this sorry scheme of things," and remolding it "nearer to the heart's desire." But the least critical examination must show that the second urge is practically equivalent to the first, and that both are aspects of the fundamental romanticism of human nature. This is undoubtedly a noble quality—provided its promptings are not taken at all literally and seriously as a guide to action. The wish of a man to be free from institutions is much like the wish of the fabled bird to be free from the existence of air, so as to be able to fly with unlimited speed. Human life, in solitude, is unthinkable and self-contradictory, and society without institutions is practically as much so. In fact, individual freedom even in relation to nature must be narrowly limited to be real or conceivable. Ultimately, freedom consists in the ability to change one's self, and must be an activity of a self with substantial existence; and it also means the freedom, and the power, to change one's world, which must similarly have substantial reality, hence stability. Thus, incidentally, the notion of omnipotence is doubly a self-contradiction. With respect to change, candid introspection will reveal to anyone that he has very little capacity to imagine either a different self, a different society, or a different physical world, which he would really expect to like better than those he already has to deal with. Certainly, no one would want to live in a society composed of people made to his own order and subject to remaking at will.

Moreover, it is obvious that the members of any society must agree with respect to its institutional structure, which means the kind of society it is and is to be, and they must agree freely if it is to be a free society, and this fact imposes even narrower bounds upon the possibilities of change. In a rational view, individual freedom in group life involves an antinomy. To behave rationally, in any activity involving others, the individual must know what behavior to expect of others; that is, for one to be rationally free, all others involved in any relationship to his activity must be mechanistically determined. The possibility of social freedom is therefore limited to rational consensus, which, as we have seen, requires agreement upon values. But, happily, the freedom of the good life is not strictly a matter of rationality in any sense, still less of instrumental rationality.

The restricting and constraining power of institutions is a fact of wide ramifications. The most literal freedom of anarchy is possible or can be approximated in associative life only in groups of extremely small size and of the most casual nature and aims. And even the most casual association—aimless sociability, conversation, and play—is seen on reflection to be far from acting in a moral vacuum. Every association is rather highly organized, with an implicit code of rules or law which must be available. This is even more the case with intellectual discussion—i.e., "serious" social intercourse—and in more formal play. And, even in the freest intercourse, problems constantly arise due to conflicts of interest and the need to resolve these without disrupting the group and sacrificing its common interests. In intellectual discussion, for example, it is constantly necessary to compromise between the interests of those who want to be heard and of those who wish to listen to those with something to say which is in some way worth attention.

Any group or association of substantial size will necessarily be organized around interests which call for some degree of stability in the association, and such a group necessarily involves much coercion of its members. There must always be a large measure of compromise between individual freedom and other values functioning as ends in group life. For actual human beings hold opinions and cherish aims in action which are more or less individual in content and more or less conflicting and competitive. Such men do not spontaneously agree on the objectives or the rules and conditions of association. The burning questions which confront modern society and threaten its destruction arise in political and economic organization. The principles involved are not essentially different from those involved in play and culture, and even in religion—in the noneconomic aspects (however, these may be defined) of these activities. It should be evident that the conditions of modern life set fairly narrow limits to the possibility of freedom for the individual either to depart from or to change the established patterns of activity, for most of these involve relationships with others, whom he cannot know personally and can with great difficulty consult, but who will be vitally affected.

The supreme concrete example of permanent and stable and large-scale grouping is, of course, the "sovereign state," defined in modern times by territorial boundaries. Living together, under the conditions of modern civilization, requires association—in particular economic co-operation—under stable forms. The co-operation is more intimate and complex between geographic neighbors, but is still "essential" between individuals and groups over an area which practically includes the world. And this also effectively applies to cultural relationships, partly because these are inseparable from those classed as economic, but also for larger reasons. It is inevitable that the world be divided up into a complex hierarchy of territorial jurisdictions, and the accidents of history and the facts of human nature have given us a political world map which few people would defend as ideal but which it is practically impossible to change extensively or rapidly without ruinously destructive war. For reasons which need not be considered here the individual actually has very little effective freedom even to choose his place of residence and his citizenship among the limited number of national states into which the earth is divided.

Moreover, within each state there is an unlimited number and variety of more or less voluntary associations along lines of special economic and cultural and other interests, to which the individual is virtually "forced" to belong, as a condition of participating in the benefits of civilization. Of paramount importance for vast numbers has come to be his inclusion in some large-scale productive enterprise. Within his state, and other associations or societies, the individual is "bound" by the existing law and by the limitations of his power to secure the consent of the other members of the group to change the law, where he does not like it as it is, and he frequently does not. In large groups the difficulty of effective intercommunication increases at an increasing rate and soon makes any close approximation to literal democracy a mathematical impossibility. These facts, particularly the conflict between freedom and concrete substantive values and ends of action, set the social problems which must be surveyed in the next chapter on the conditions necessary for realizing the ideal of freedom.

# IV

# THE IDEAL OF FREEDOM: CONDITIONS FOR ITS REALIZATION

FRANK H. KNIGHT

THIS chapter will naturally be a continuation of the preceding one. The meaning of an ideal or objective cannot be sharply separated from the conditions and the modes of action relevant to its realization. The previous chapter should have made it clear that, in our present culture situation, the problem of action under the guidance of freedom as an ideal cannot be discussed without constant and careful regard to wide differences in the meanings which the word bears, both in popular discussion and in the writings of social theorists and philosophers. We pointed out in particular that the term "freedom" has become a symbol for nearly everything that human beings think they want and do not have, and which, consequently, as they infer, it must be somebody's obligation to supply. Of course, people demand only what they claim a right to have, but the difference they make between this and what they regard as needful, or even what they strongly desire, is commonly less than would be made by an impartial spectator.

A fine illustration of the intellectual confusion with respect to the meaning of freedom which reigns in current social discussion is at hand in the enumeration of the "Four Freedoms," recently promulgated by President Roosevelt as the goal to be achieved in national and world reorganization after the present war. The list undoubtedly sums up, with the author's usual political astuteness, the things of which the great mass of the people feel themselves unjustly deprived in the social-psychological situation of prolonged economic crisis, followed by a war between "democracy" and "dictatorship" as types or principles of social order. Mr. Roosevelt's list, as you will recall, includes freedom of expression, freedom of worship, freedom from want, and freedom from fear.

The statement is so naïve that it smacks of unkindness to ask what any of these freedoms has to do with freedom or what it means or what are the conditions or possibilities of its realization—specifically by democratic political agencies. One of its most conspicuous features, in the light of quite recent history, is the absence of any reference to most of the traditional freedoms of economic and political liberalism. There is nothing to suggest freedom in the consumption, exchange, or production of goods or services, or freedom of the individual to make provision for the future, his own or that of his family—and, in fact, no reference is made to any aspect of freedom in family life. Nor is there any mention of the concrete freedoms of democracy, the right to vote in the selection of the personnel of government and to hold political office.

Doubtless all these rights are taken for granted. But the more serious criticism is that nothing is said about the corresponding obligations, or the limitations or necessary conditions, which are obviously present, and in which all the real problems lie. Even freedom of expression is meaningless apart from a right to be listened to, and is likely to be taken to mean the right of an individual to be heard and heeded by his fellow-citizens as a body, a "freedom" which is mathematically impossible for any considerable number. Similar strictures apply to freedom of worship, which is hardly at issue with respect to private worship (the form originally enjoined on Christians), or apart from the right of some to prescribe and enforce forms of religious service for others. Freedom to organize worship may easily cloak an assumed right to build up a political machine or "party," with a view to controlling the state. There is no boundary between religious and other interests, and we are reminded that in American history, not so remote, the Latter Day Saints were prohibited by federal action from practicing a fundamental tenet of their religion, even in a sovereign state which they had founded and politically controlled. Freedom from want, again, is without content unless it means a right to be taken care of by someone with the necessary means, and whose freedom is surely affected by this obligation. And it is assumed without question that someone will have the means to take care of everybody, when such an obligation is attached to the fruits of production and accumulation. Throughout modern history, the right of anyone in acute want to relief has been unquestioned, subject to limits and conditions believed to be necessary, and the only possible issue has to do with these limits and conditions. Finally, freedom from fear suggests even more obvious questions as to what obligations are to be imposed, and how, and at what sacrifice of other freedoms or rights.[1]

As a preliminary to the main argument, it will be well to summarize briefly the main distinctions in the meaning of freedom in connection with our purposes which were devel-

[1] The writer would have supposed it to be clear without more explicit statement than is given in the text that these paragraphs about the "Four Freedoms" are illustrative and are used for that reason, and in particular that they represent no criticism of this particular specimen of the "manifesto" type of political document. Such writing would never be heard of, unless to be ridiculed, if its use of language did not place popular appeal and emotive power ahead of analytic accuracy. Under less pressure of space limits, this point might have received more development, perhaps with the addition of other illustrations. This note is added in view of a criticism offered by a distinguished political scientist who read the lecture as it was going through the press. The critic construes this section as "a rather unjustifiable attack against President Roosevelt's four freedoms," attributes it to the writer's "tendency to abstraction" and his "unawareness" that similar matter has long been common in bills of rights. All this may be significant as a further illustration of the main theme of chapters iii and iv—the way in which language is used, and understood, in political discussion.

oped in the preceding chapter. We distinguished first between three ultimate general conceptions, corresponding to the religious or mystical (or quietistic), the romantic, and the modern liberal views of life. Both the first and the second of these mean essentially freedom from responsibility in thinking and action. In the religious view, this state is to be achieved by "accepting the universe"—either suppressing all desire, or bringing it into harmony with what God or fate or the Absolute in some meaning may send, and so achieving serenity and peace. In a thoroughgoing form, this means annihilation, at least as far as earthly life is concerned. At the practicable limit at which individual and social life could go on, it means the contemplative life, thinking without acting, which is possible only for a limited number of individuals living parasitically within a society pursuing a more or less antithetical ideal, or perhaps realizing this one vicariously. At the opposite extreme, romanticism means acting without thinking— "thinking with the blood." In this direction, also, some compromise is necessary to avoid destruction. Acceptance of some responsibility is a condition of life itself. The conception of freedom in the modern view of life allows the individual the widest range of choice in compromising between the two extremes but inculcates quite definitely a middle ground. Spiritual freedom is to be achieved through knowing and accepting the limiting conditions of activity and choosing intelligently among the alternatives open, while the substance of reasonable romanticism, an interesting life, is to be realized through free constructive activity within the possible limits. The ultimate end or purpose is worth-while achievement in the form of individual growth and social progress. Our discussion of the conditions necessary for realizing freedom will run entirely in terms of this third conception, defined by the modern ethical world view.

We pointed out that in social relations freedom is necessarily restricted and largely defined by moral responsibility, and especially by law, customary and juridic, as a condition necessary for orderly social life. The free individual must live in a free society, in which his sphere of literally free activity is defined by such law, itself made by the free and equal participation of all members of society, and representing an intellectual-moral consensus as to the content of rights and obligations. Social freedom, under law, is essentially a negative concept; it means freedom from interference in individual activity, except for the limitations of law of the character stated. Ideally, it means free association, based on rational mutual consent in all relationships—i.e., freedom not to associate unless the terms are acceptable. The practical problem centers in the necessary legal restrictions, or the right scope and content of law, and in the democratic character of the state as the agency by which a society makes and enforces law. In general usage, the concept of freedom has been illogically extended to include the right to possess and control the means or power without which action is of course impossible. We suggested, as a compromise, calling this right "effective freedom." In a defensible use of terms, it is the right to power and not to freedom. Ideal social relations undoubtedly include also some right to assistance, to relief of want or suffering, and to security, subject to reasonable conditions; but it is merely confusing to bring all such rights under the conception of freedom.

Turning now to the subject of the present lecture, it should be obvious that, ideally, the conditions requisite for realizing the ideal of freedom in any society are intellectual and moral qualities in its members. The ultimate ideal (in an absolute, not a realistic, sense) is anarchy, in which the only law is the moral law, recognized—i.e., rationally agreed upon—by every individual, and needing no enforcement. Progress toward this ideal, from the present undeveloped and "sinful" state of man, as well as the maintenance of such civilization as the race has achieved, is possible only through social action involving compulsion. Ideally, again, at a first remove from the ultimate ideal, social action would doubtless take the form of intellectual and moral education, chiefly if not exclusively in childhood. This statement, however, leaves the conception of freedom ambiguous. The content of law might still be such as to realize freedom—in the sense that men would feel free—through conditioning the will, eliminating desire or bringing it into conformity with actuality, rather than by providing the conditions of free activity. And we must constantly keep in mind the fact that from the standpoint of social peace—which is always a primary consideration, and a necessity within limits—it is this feeling of freedom, based on acceptance of things as they are, to the extent of eliminating destructive expression of discontent, which is in question. If men are to be free, they must be educated and habituated to self-discipline, at least to the extent of not struggling to achieve the impossible or to have benefits without paying the necessary cost; and this is just as obviously a condition of their being reasonably "happy." In our cultural situation, the danger lies in the direction of romanticism, of demanding the impossible, which actually threatens catastrophe and destruction, specifically through war. Excessive quietism would finally be equally destructive, but in an entirely different way, and human nature as we see it around us is not inclined toward that extreme.

Thus the immediate practical problem is in fact primarily one of intellectual and moral education. The public must be made to understand vastly better than it does the possibilities and limitations of life, particularly of life in organized society, and the possibilities and limitations of action directed toward its improvement. But the requirement of moral education is in a sense even prior to that of intellectual. Men must first of all have the disposition to act in the light of knowledge and to acquire the necessary knowledge and understanding. They must be cured of the age-old inveterate romanticism, which has found expression in the practices of magic, and especially of witchcraft—the disposition to explain all supposed evils by finding some malevolent agent, preferably some human being or group, and to resort to punishment or "liquidation" as a remedy. This disposition doubtless finds its primary exemplification in the history of "medicine," the treatment of disease. Even in the most civilized societies the development of a really objective scientific attitude toward these problems, in the mass of the population, is still largely to be achieved. Actual witchcraft has, to be sure, been largely eliminated, but beliefs and practices essentially at the level of superstition undoubtedly still predominate over science, except as the latter is directly enforced by law.

The natural man is still a romantic, disposed to act without much regard for rational knowledge and thought. He is still what has been called a "Gawdsaker"; his maxim is "for God's sake, do something!" Apart from witchcraft, what men have always typically done when they were ill is to take some poison; if they recovered, it was attributed to the treatment, and if they did not, it was held to be because they did not take enough, or because some detail was wrong. In the field of social maladies, the progress made toward superseding this attitude with action based upon rational investigation is small, in comparison even with the field of individual medicine. We must assume as the basis of any discussion that the masses of men are potentially intelligent enough not to strike out blindly against the inevitable, not to act rashly and therefore destructively, or even to make themselves acutely unhappy about what demonstrably cannot be helped. Otherwise, we must admit in advance that free society is an impossibility, and give up the problem as hopeless. No cure for the ills of society is to be found in blind resort to conflict against some supposed enemy, until he can be shown to be really to blame, or in the equally romantic impulse to take the machinery of social organization to pieces and rebuild it, without an understanding of the mechanism and of the functions to be performed by the social order and the problems which are involved.

By way of approach to the problem of freedom in and through social organization under law, it will be useful to classify individual and social interests and activities along psychological lines, under the three heads of work, play, and culture. With specific reference to our topic, play and work are commonly thought of as virtually synonymous, respectively, with free and unfree or compulsory activity, while cultural pursuits are more or less intermediate, combining the features of work and play. However, examination somewhat surprisingly shows that all these activities are structurally much alike, and that even the psychological contrast in men's feelings toward them hardly stands up under critical examination. All three involve the use of means and the economy of means, in realizing ends which the acting subject "wants" to achieve. The reasons why he wants to achieve them also analyze into the same list of basic human desires, urges, or interests—a vague mixture of "needs" for life and comfort and for satisfactory growth or development, merging into desires for things or types of experience viewed as less important. All are very largely socially conditioned; their content is a matter of social psychology and culture history. As already noted, the scientific problem of analyzing these desires and dispositions, and the social problem of giving them the right content, are very difficult to discuss, and we must here take them as given, until near the close of the chapter.

The meaning of work and play is a strangely neglected sub-

ject and some comparison will be necessary to bring out the
facts which are essential for understanding the feeling of
unfreedom. As will be shown presently, the notion of work
must be extended to cover all economic endeavor, regardless
of the relation between labor and external means used in the
activity. The least inspection of what is superficially classed
as work shows that physical subsistence and comfort play a
minor role in the motivation, while recreation is also necessary to comfort and even to health, and shows also that no
sharp contrast exists even in terms of enjoyment. The real motive in both production and consumption is largely competition, emulation, or rivalry, which is also the characteristic
source of interest in play. Work and play are clearly instrumental to each other, as is true of all the elements in "the good
life," whatever elements may be distinguished. The psychological motivation of all activities must be provisionally described in some such terms as the famous "four wishes" of
W. I. Thomas—adventure, security, recognition, and response
—which tell us nothing about concrete content. In particular,
all are competitive or involve emulation. To the list should
undoubtedly be added the quest for power—as an end, not as
a means—and "development," along right or approved lines,
will be found to be the ultimate end in all cases, in so far as the
activity is rational. But the concrete meaning of all these
terms depends almost entirely on the social-cultural or historical situation.

The most important fact is that all three kinds of activity—
work, play, and culture—present the combination of harmony
and conflict of interests which we emphasized in the previous
chapter as the basis and presupposition of the existence of any
social or group problem, and of the need for law. Moreover,
the problem of law in relation to freedom arises in essentially
the same form in all our three fields of associative action. Play
as well as work must have its law, the rules of the game, es-

pecially if socially organized, as it usually is, though there is no ultimate or profound distinction between social play and solitaire. In all cases, laws can be discussed only in intellectual terms, not those of mere individual desire. The social-ethical problem of "fair" play may easily be viewed in the same terms as that of economic life—i.e., "justice" in the assignment of roles and the distribution of the fruits of activity in relation to the effort and "capacity" employed in the game.

The psychological difference between play and work, the feeling of freedom versus compulsion, seems to lie in conditions which in the case of work bring about a relatively sharp separation between the activity and the result aimed at, a separation between "production" and "consumption." These conditions will be taken up presently. In play the activity and the achievement run closer together, and the interest seems to center more in the activity; the result seems to be arbitrarily set up as an end, in order to make the activity interesting, whereas the feeling about work involves the converse relation, the activity is instrumental to the result. (The means-end relationship in general is elusive, and this has been too much emphasized in recent thought to call for development here, even if space allowed.)

The psychology of work—specifically, the feeling of compulsion in the mind of the "free" worker—seems to be largely a peculiar product of advanced civilization. Among primitive peoples the contrast between work and play is certainly far less developed, if they have it at all. And the higher animals almost certainly do not have it to any extent, though we distinguish some of their activities, chiefly in infancy (in the wild state), as play. Incidentally, the economically rational man, all of whose ends were given, not problematic (the "economic man"), would not work and would hardly play, as he would be interested only in tangible results, and in particular would not experience competitive motivation. It is the work attitude which is especially distinctive of man, and more especially of modern civilized man, and this peculiar feeling of unfreedom in economic life sets our main social problem. But the philosophically more important fact is the tendency of work interests to dissolve under critical scrutiny into those of play, and specifically into competitive emulation—"keeping up with the Jones's," or keeping or getting ahead of them. The weakness of the economic view of activity is precisely in the fact that it takes ends as given, while for critical thought the immediate ends always resolve themselves into means, and the interest in ends in turn largely dissolves into unreality or into a play interest.

However, there are also "real" ends in economic activity. The "standard of living," which is for the most part aesthetic in content, represents the content of civilization and the difference between human and animal life. It is the combination of these real ends or values with the play interest and other activity interests which makes the social-economic problem at once difficult and interesting. If we inquire further into the ultimate ends, the values of civilized life, we shall find culture and cultural growth in the individual, and progress in society, the provisional answer to the question in the case of both work and play. It is more natural to raise the question of ends with respect to work, but we do ask it about play also, especially in ranking and choosing games. Culture, again, analyzes into the familiar triad of values, truth, beauty, and goodness, or intellectual, aesthetic, and moral experience and progress, while recreative enjoyment is as much a part of the good life as are its "serious" ends. In order to carry further the investigation into the purposive free life, we must consider in more detail the relation between means and ends, in connection with work, and the meaning of economic activity, which we have been taking for granted.

All the primary aspects of freedom as a defensible ideal—freedom to act, but to act responsibly (meaning the right use of power), and "effective" freedom as the right to have power—point directly to the concept of economic freedom as the central problem in the politico-legal order. The meaning of that concept must now be indicated more precisely than was done in the previous chapter. In a broad, logical sense it includes all freedom, since economy is a universal aspect of rational behavior or conduct. And even in the narrow definition in terms of monetary activities—buying and selling, which is virtually the meaning in popular usage—it is in the economic field that the feeling of unfreedom has given rise to serious problems in our society in recent times. It is in relation to the aspect of the state as an instrument in connection with economic relations that our problems center in politics and political action. Intelligent purposive behavior always involves the more or less effective use of power, or means, to realize ends. Economy is merely a synonym for efficiency, or effectiveness, and the effort to be effective makes every problem to some extent an economic problem. This is only one part of the problem of conduct, its "economic aspect"; the other part is selection among concrete ends in terms of final or noninstrumental values. The economic view takes the ends as given—i.e., as already decided upon. But the social problem as it arises in political life centers in the individual provision and use of means, and that phase of it will logically be considered first and primarily. In modern society men do not feel unfree in the selection of ends, except as this choice is conditioned by the available means and restrictions upon their use.

To avoid confusion as to the nature of the problem of economic freedom, one must be on guard against two major fallacies which pervade popular thinking and political agitation. The first is the notion that there is a distinct class of economic ends—specifically, that provision for the "higher" wants is not just as much an economic problem as provision for the "lower" or for the "animal" needs. As every literate adult really knows, what we call the necessaries or subsistence requirements in any social-cultural setting are overwhelmingly a matter of conformity to "standards" of "decency," which are aesthetic and social in content. In fact, it is the higher wants which are the more expensive, as pointed out in our first chapter. The second fallacy is that of thinking of economic means in terms of physical materials and implements, or "property" in the ordinary meaning of the term, in contrast with human beings themselves. In fact, some three-fourths of the productive capacity used in the United States, measured in money value, consists of human abilities. Analytically speaking, the human being himself, the individual's own person, is a "means of production" in much the same sense as any external material or instrument. Useful human capacities are also "artificial"; they are the product of previous economic activity, as completely as any machine or device more typically called a "capital good." And the same is true of what are called "natural resources." These three traditional "factors of production," as they exist and are used at any time, are all the result of the previous transformation of materials ultimately derived from nature, but which in their natural state would not be useful for the purposes of civilized life and would have no economic value. They present no differences in essential principle; all are "capital" in the correct definition of that concept. The human being in particular, as he comes into the world from the hands of "nature," is an economic liability, not an asset. He becomes a useful agent through a process of investment, made in him by others and by himself, which is not different in principle from that involved in the construction of a manufacturing plant, or of any tool or instrument.

From the economic point of view, the really distinctive feature of human life—which is to say civilized life—is not that men rationally use means; this is also true of the higher animals, in varying degrees and ways. What is distinctive of man is that the means used (human and material) exist in a highly transformed state, and that if such life is to continue this artificial "equipment" must constantly be maintained and replaced, through rationally planned activity involving all the means already at hand. Human society uses a stock or fund of "productive capacity"—embodied in human beings and external physical things—which has been accumulated through historical time from the dim evolutionary beginnings of human life. This stock has been maintained and increased (of course with notable recessions, as civilizations have developed and decayed) through the use of the stock in existence at any time in such a way as to increase the total, in addition to yielding its primary "product," a flow of consumable services. The social stock of productive capacity must not only be maintained if civilized life is to continue, but must be further increased if civilization is to be progressive—and it will almost certainly decay if it does not progress. Economic conduct and the problem of economic freedom refer simply to the economic aspect of life-activity, the economic or economically rational use of means, regardless of kind, for the realization of ends, also regardless of kind, but taken as given or already decided upon. But the end must include the maintenance and increase of the means, or there will be no sense in thinking about the future at all. This provision for maintenance and growth must, of course, be socially continuous. If it is to be effected by individuals, their interests in action must look beyond their individual lives.

Economic activity, as free, consequently has three "dimensions": It involves (*a*) choice, based on purely quantitative comparison, among partial or provisional ends for which means are to be used, the different given "wants" to be satisfied in consumption; (*b*) choice among concrete modes of using means, the technique or technology to be employed; and (*c*) decision as to the amount of means to be used in maintaining or increasing the stock of means itself, the human and material capital of the individual and of society. In all of these fields of activity all kinds of means, human and nonhuman, function in a complementary way and constitute an integral or organic unit, the social capital. It should now be clear why the concept of work must be extended to include all conduct in its economic, or economically rational, aspect.

The ultimate unity of all forms of purposive action—work, play, and culture—with reference to the problem of social organization, may be visualized by imagining the conditions of life so changed that the economic problem would no longer exist. The result is somewhat disturbing, in the face of the fact that work is primitively (and religiously) thought of as the primal curse of human life. If we imagine that men were granted the ability to perform physical miracles, say by some supernatural power, or by the discovery of a magical process which would work, so that all economic production could be carried out simply by wishing, the social problem would not be solved and probably not alleviated or even changed in form. In the abstract, it is at least as arguable that it would be greatly intensified, and destructive conflict made correspondingly more difficult to avoid—unless play and culture (and social and religious) interests were at the same time so transformed that men themselves would cease to be recognizable as human.

The reasons for the work feeling, so characteristic of economic production in modern life—and which as irksome effort is not very different between property-owners and those who live by labor—are connected with the choice both of ends and of means. The roots of the compulsive power of the urge to maintain a relatively expensive standard of living have already been suggested; it is partly a matter of the awakening of taste in the masses, and partly one of psychological competition, emulation, and rivalry, and it cannot be probed more deeply here. In any case, the feeling of unfreedom undoubtedly arises to a greater extent on the side of means, as a consequence of obvious features of the production process. This has become at the same time highly mechanized on a vast scale and relatively precarious in its operation. It involves a large and intricate human organization based on impersonal relations, with the necessity of operating continuously. An individual, or a personal group, has little ability to make changes without disastrous consequences to itself and others. It is an obvious feature of organized relations that changes made by one member disrupt the plans and conditions of life of the others, unless all changes are worked out and preconcerted in advance on the basis of the explicit consent of all.

In any case, the fact remains that the social problem in our civilization centers very largely in what people call "economic unfreedom." The bulk of our substantive law has to do with economic life, and economic problems and relationships form the subject matter of most of our political discussion, by the general public and in our legislatures. The task of the philosophic analyst becomes that of explaining this fact, and of indicating to the statesman or politician the true nature of the problem, so that he may work intelligently at his practical task of finding appropriate measures for dealing with it. To attack the former task we must start with two facts as given. The first is that men have individual interests which take the form of realizing ends, achievement of which is narrowly restricted by scarcity of the means available, so that they are impelled to the economy of means, and also to efforts to increase the available total stock of means, the productive capacity or economic power under their control. The second fact is that the efficiency of these "economic" endeavors can be almost infinitely increased by entering into mutually instrumental social relationships of co-operation or organization, which at the same time involve direct conflicts of interest. The practically unlimited increase in efficiency involved is undoubtedly a main factor in causing organized activity to be felt as compulsory. In the present stage of civilization, unorganized or self-sufficient economic life would at best mean a standard of living which would be felt to be intolerable, even for a greatly reduced population.

In fact, of course, no one proposes that. The sense of unfreedom, and the discontent and protest, express themselves rather in a clamor for radical change in the *form* of economic organization. Consequently, our first main inquiry should center in a study of the existent form, from the standpoint of freedom and unfreedom. It should attempt to learn why the individual has so much the feeling of being coerced, how far this feeling corresponds with facts, how far proposed changes in the economic system, or any feasible changes, offer a substantial opportunity for increasing real freedom—or the real values which are called by that name—without intolerable loss of effectiveness, or how far the problem is one of dispelling illusion and mere romantic discontent, as already suggested. Such an inquiry must lead to the conclusion that the discontent with the form of economic organization is in fact based almost entirely on misconception and wishful or prejudiced thinking, or feeling rather than thinking—what I am calling romanticism. But this does not mean that there is no basis for action, that the solution of the social problem is merely to teach men to accept things as they are and be content. The true conclusion, indeed, is partly that expectations and demands commonly have little relation to possibilities, but, further, that the treatment advocated is wrong because the diagnosis is wrong—if, indeed, it should be dignified by the name of diagnosis at all. The inquiry itself cannot be carried out in the compass of a chapter; obviously it would call for a treatise on economics, as a first

step. All that we can do is very briefly to run over the ground,
list a few of the main results to which the investigation would
lead—with a brevity which must make our statements seem
dogmatic—and contrast them with the fallacious and romantic notions commonly held by the public.

In a liberal economic order, such as was approximated in
this country in the latter part of the nineteenth century, the
terms of association are defined by the prices of goods and
services, determined by purchase and sale in markets, described as "freely" competitive. The first "romantic misconception" which calls for notice centers in the use of this term
"competition" to describe the market and the market organization of economic life. Transactions in an effective market involve no psychological competition whatever, and on
this point the facts are very largely in conformity with the
theory, as every literate adult really knows. The meaning of a
market is simply that a plurality of individuals are in a relationship of effective intercommunication, in which each is
"free" to offer terms of exchange to any other and to accept
or refuse the terms offered by any other. As soon as a market
is established as a going concern, it results in fixing a system
of prices which are virtually objective, as far as any individual
is concerned. The freedom of any individual consists in choosing on the basis of established prices what commodities he
will produce and sell, and in what quantities, and which ones
he will buy and consume. Where goods or services are produced for exchange under rational economic motivation—i.e.,
for the satisfaction of given wants of the producer—the whole
operation is to be understood in terms of the comparative efficiency of different methods of production. An economically
rational subject produces one thing and exchanges it for another if and because he gets a greater value or "satisfaction"
by so doing. That is, he either gets a greater quantity of the

same good, or a more desirable good, than he could secure by using his productive powers directly, in a self-sufficient way, to satisfy his wants. In producing for exchange he is still in effect using his own resources in his own way to satisfy his own wants. In terms of motives, he is behaving on exactly the same principles as a Crusoe, choosing between different modes of using his productive capacity so as to secure the maximum benefits in quantity and kind of results.

Thus what is called market competition is really a purely technological and impersonal category. Viewed in the large it is a method of organizing co-operation in the interest of increasing the effectiveness of activity where both means and ends are given an individual. And in a system of co-operation organized in this way, every individual enjoys complete social freedom; he is free in the sense in which a Crusoe is free (more accurately, in the sense in which a Crusoe would be free if he operated a productive mechanism with the mechanical characteristics of the modern economic order). As stated before, everyone really knows that there is in the buying and selling transactions of ordinary life substantially no psychological competition, and no exercise of persuasive power in the way of "bargaining." He also knows that the prices are fixed by impersonal conditions, which are beyond the control of the other party, as of himself, whether he is buying groceries in a retail store, selling agricultural products to a local trader, or selling his labor to an employer. Yet he commonly alleges the contrary, because he feels unfree. The typical human being, the educated as well as the uneducated, shows an inveterate tendency to assume that because he does not decide the terms of exchange, or influence them by fiat, someone else must be dictating to him arbitrarily. In essence, the attitude represents a survival of the animistic ideas with which primitive man, unable to conceive of objective fact, viewed the world as a whole, inanimate as well as animate nature. The first step in getting men to feel free is to get them to apply the knowledge they already possess, to take a rational or objective attitude, instead of a romantic one, toward the conditions of their lives. Otherwise they not only will be unhappy, but are certain to act in ways which are destructive instead of remedial.

It is true that real economic relations are largely competitive, in the psychological sense, as we have already emphasized. But this has nothing whatever to do with the form of organization. It is true for the same reason that other social relations are competitive, specifically our play, in which we feel especially free. It is because human nature is competitive and competition seems to be necessary to make any activity interesting. But psychological competition is alien to economic motivation, as already noted, and in the effective market the individual behaves as an economic man. In so far as he does so behave, the market organization both involves perfect liberty and enables each participant to achieve the maximum gain in efficiency which is to be had through mutually free specialization and co-operation. He could improve his position only through one-sided transfers at the expense of others, predation or gift, or through placing his own affairs in the hands of someone more competent than himself to manage them. Incidentally, the free-market economy leaves individuals free to make this arrangement on mutually agreeable terms, and it is a common occurrence. It is to be noted, too, that if any two parties dislike for any reason the "objective" terms fixed by the general give-and-take, they are free to deal on any other terms upon which they may agree—specifically, to set a "fair" price if they think the market price is unjustly high or low. And, further, if any "society" is convinced that the terms of the free market give some individuals too little and others too much, it is free to take from some for the benefit of others, by taxation, or to regulate or suppress any form of trade, without changing the system of organization.

All this, however, as we have already stated, does not mean either that the free-market economy has produced ideal results in reality, or that there is no chance for improvement through social action. On the other side of the case, the side of rational criticism, inquiry would naturally proceed in two stages. First, we should have to investigate the relations between the perfect competition of theory and actual conditions; and, second, we should look into the matter of diagnosis of the evils in terms other than the form of organization. Under the first head, it goes without saying that the actual functioning of the market mechanism is not in strict conformity with the theoretical pattern. This is not even true of physical machines, and far less so of any mechanism of human organization. With reference to the economic organization, it should be evident that individuals have much to gain by breaking the rules, and that the competitive-market ideal will not be realized or approximated without a large amount of intelligent social action through the making and enforcement of appropriate rules or laws. This is the first and main practical problem, whether social policy should in general be directed toward making competition effective or to discarding the system outright and replacing it with one of an entirely different pattern. The second course will naturally be advisable only if another pattern can be found which will be really better, on the whole. (It is a paradoxical but evident truth that for practical purposes a hopeless situation is identical with an ideal one.)

We can only run over in a most cursory manner a few criticisms, of what may be called a mechanical sort, which are brought against the free-market organization and are supposed to justify its rejection. No doubt the two most common allegations treated as conclusive by the romantic critics are, first, that competition is an economic myth of theorists or a fable used to dupe the unwary in the interest of exploiters, that the business economy is and must be dominated by monopoly; and, second, that it is in the nature of such a system to fall into cyclical oscillations, and particularly into periodic depressions, so disastrous as to make the system intolerable.

On the first point, monopoly, we can only make a few assertions, without giving the facts or arguments to support them. The amount of monopoly actually present is grossly exaggerated in the popular mind, and the nature and causes of monopoly and its evils grossly misunderstood. A considerable amount of monopoly is not merely unpreventable, and in that sense a part of the cost of freedom and progress, but is functionally necessary. This should be clear from the case of patents on inventions, and similar legal devices, and from the evident fact that monopoly which is not based on deliberate public grant functions in the same way: the hope for a temporary monopoly gain serves as the incentive to experimentation and development. Such gains may be, and in fact are, offset or more than offset by losses incurred in similar activities and must be viewed as the earned reward of taking risks which are inevitable in a progressive society. Moreover, the evils of monopoly are very largely the product of unwise governmental action or are the indirect result of depression conditions. The public, however, seems to think that the remedy for monopoly is more monopoly, deliberately set up in favor of the groups (primarily wage-earners and farmers) which feel themselves victimized by the largely imaginary monopolies of "big business" and "high finance." This assumes that the way to have more, all around, is to produce less.

With respect to the business cycle, it must suffice here to point out two facts. The first is that practically no one makes any gain out of depression; and, in particular, that the owners of business enterprises suffer enormous losses, including wholesale bankruptcy. Consequently, the problem is twofold: the scientific one of discovering the cause and devising appropriate remedies, and the application of the remedies when found—a matter of the political competence of democracy. The second observation, which must also stand as an assertion, is that any "planned" economy which seriously attempted to preserve the fundamental liberties of individuals would embody the same tendencies and encounter the same difficulties. For the roots of cyclical tendencies are to be found in the money-and-credit mechanism; and the socialistic planners do not propose to eliminate purchase and sale in terms of money as the general pattern of economic organization—and certainly could not do so without making the mere administrative task insuperable.

Passing over other more or less appealing lines of argument, the general conclusion must be that the first objective in a social policy aimed at the maximum individual freedom must be to make competition reasonably effective where it is not—and in any case to make it as effective as possible in the great bulk of the productive organization. In exceptional cases, where this is not feasible—such as the "natural monopolies" (chiefly public utilities)—the procedure indicated is to substitute public enterprise, governmental ownership and operation. All price control must be pronounced bad, for whatever reason it is employed (though emergencies, especially war, produce conditions under which there seems to be no alternative). The possible alternative to the price economy would be some political system of controlling production and distribution, some form of planned economy, or collectivism or socialism. But, as we have seen, socialists do not propose to get away from the market organization as the basic pattern of their system. Passing over grave doubts as to whether the two mechanisms, business and politics, could be effectively combined, there is every reason against believing that political machinery would in practice conform any more closely to its theoretical principles, or come nearer to realizing its ideal objective. Reasoning from known facts and principles indicates that collectivism would aggravate the very evils of the system which is miscalled "capitalism" which it would be particularly intended to cure. And, in addition, a little reflection should make it clear that any government faced with the task of ordering the economic affairs of a modern nation, to say nothing of world relations, would necessarily be a dictatorship, suppressing personal liberty in all fields of social life as well as the distinctively economic. If theoretical arguments on these points left any room for reasonable doubt, the course of events in the European world since the first World War, and specifically the Russian experiment, should be sufficient to remove them.

The issue with respect to the open-market economic order, as already stated, is correct diagnosis, in place of the false one that competition does not work, that it is a "myth" and cannot be realized. The root fallacy is the idea that the complete realization of economic freedom would solve or eliminate the major social problems. It rests on a confusion between freedom and power—or, in a more comprehensive view, on the mistake of taking the individual as given, with respect both to his endowment with economic power and to his wants or dispositions (what he desires to do with power and freedom).

The first step which must be taken as a prerequisite for the intelligent discussion of power in economic relations is to separate analytically economic power in the form in which it appears in the free market from other forms. In an effectively competitive market organization, economic power consists exclusively of the productive capacity which the individual possesses, including personal capacity or labor power and the ownership of external wealth or property. It is a matter of individual sharing in the aggregate social capital—and, of course, of the total amount of that capital, relative to population, accumulated down to any given time. Productive capacity is measured by its economic value, which depends upon the demand of other persons as consumers for the ultimate product. And this demand is made up of two factors, consumers' desires or preferences and their economic capacity, which is their source of purchasing power.

The second step (which might, indeed, have been placed first) is to recognize both that economic power is sadly limited in comparison with human needs (in contrast with the nonsense we hear about poverty in the midst of abundance), and that there is an inherent conflict between freedom and power. For power is indefinitely multiplied by organization, while effective organization reduces individual freedom. Men have to choose as to how far they wish to give up freedom for power in production—or, more accurately, for increased effective freedom as consumers, a higher standard of living, and wider choice in its composition.

Without carrying the analysis further, it should be clear that no intelligent discussion of economic problems, in terms of freedom and power, is possible without a clear understanding of the mechanical and functional relationships in the market economy as a whole, the activities or roles which mutually condition one another and under the given conditions determine all prices and so the terms of association. And a second and equally necessary step must be to know what these given conditions are and to understand the way in which they change, in consequence of normal individual behavior under such conditions, before proceeding to consider how they can be changed by planned social action. Any statement made without these preliminary achievements is certain to reflect wish-thinking—either self-interest or romanticism—and if made the basis of action is certain to lead to disastrous results. Without this knowledge and understanding, reformers and agitators are simply "monkeying" with an infinitely intricate and delicate mechanism and the consequences are not in doubt.

The primary "romantic delusion" in the public mind is the

belief that a few individuals exercise enormous power and reap vast "unearned" returns through the ownership and management of business enterprise. This notion is closely connected with the ideas about monopoly already considered. To dispel the error, the objective inquirer need only look into the statistics of the distribution of income, and of the mortality (bankruptcy) among business enterprises. He will not be able to find any monopoly gain, or "profit," properly defined. All the evidence, theoretical and factual, indicates that, in the aggregate, business losses at least equal or exceed the gains, allowing for the fair value of services furnished by their owners to production. In a free and progressive economy (with antisocial practices suppressed), it is in the nature of things that some ventures will be conspicuously successful while others will fail. It is also in the nature of things that success and failure will correspond in a general way with social service, reflecting better or worse foresight or competence —but only in a general way—and that the results will be largely affected and distorted by "luck," good or bad.

We cannot go into the conditions, the facts of nature and human nature, which make it necessary for large-scale productive units to exist and to operate under the orders of a centralized directive authority. It is fairly well recognized that both large-scale organization and centralized direction are, in fact, conditions necessary to efficiency in the world as it is. In theory, production might be organized under the form of "democracy," meaning representative government, or a town meeting, or even anarchy. (In theory, an army might also be so organized!) Under the legal order of liberalism, no artificial obstacle has prevented the participants in enterprise from organizing as democratically as they might like. Various types of "economic democracy"—or, more specifically, of producers' co-operation—have been repeatedly tried by their advocates under all sorts of conditions and have usually proved unable to survive. The specific reasons are not far to seek, but are not to be recounted here. In general, the enterprise has taken the form it actually assumes (typically that of the business corporation—which *is* partially democratic) for the reason that this is the form which has proved least unsatisfactory to the individuals immediately concerned, and to society as a whole. It does involve much concentration of nominal directive or managerial authority, and some really "arbitrary" power. But any candid appraisal must lead to the verdict that the same result is at least as characteristic of any representative institutions which human beings have been able to devise and operate. One need only compare business management with politics, in any unit from the town or city to the nation, to confirm the conclusion that, between the two, market competition is more effective in compelling those who nominally exercise power to act responsibly as the agents of those whose interests they are supposed to serve. Once more, the way to possible improvement in economic organization in its mechanical aspects lies through intelligent action to make competition more effective and not through replacing business with politics, as planners and reformers advocate.

This brings us to the chief valid and serious criticism to be made against the liberal economic order, one which has little to do with the free-market form of organization. The main real problem is economic power, correctly defined, as the ownership of productive capacity. A little reflection on familiar facts will show the fallacy of the idea that even ideal market competition necessarily or naturally implies ideal or good results in the human (social and ethical) sense. The truth is quite obviously to the contrary. Productive capacity, as we have pointed out, is itself a product. The conditions under which, and methods by which, individuals acquire economic power set limits to individual freedom, properly so-called, as an ideal in social relations and organized life; and further limits are set by the way in which they get their wants, also taken as given in the mechanical analysis of the market organization. The conclusion that perfect competition would involve both maximum freedom and maximum efficiency, and ideal "justice" as between given individuals, means only that the fruits of productive activity would be distributed on the basis of the economic power (productive capacity, labor power, and property) possessed at any time by each individual, measured by the economic demand of the other members of the community. This result will not be ethically ideal, or just, in the larger sense of distributive in contrast with commutative justice, unless the distribution of productive capacity itself is ethically ideal. Or, the result would be practically ideal if this distribution were really and unalterably given, beyond improvement by social action.

But the first of these assumptions is untenable in terms of accepted modern ideals, and the second is false to the facts. The endowment of any individual with economic power at any time is the product, in part, of his own previous activity. But in larger part, and on the whole, predominantly, it is the product of the previous working of the whole economic institutional system in which the individual has lived. It is therefore predominantly due to factors beyond the individual's control, to the nature and operation of the institutional system itself, which is the primary object matter of social action. The amount of economic capacity in existence in any society at any time, and its distribution among individuals, depend on a mixture of biological and social inheritance, as well as the previous behavior of the living individuals. No one now thinks either that men are created equal or that endowment with power corresponds with desert or excellence of moral character. In a progressive society the inequitable tendencies of the factors named are further greatly affected by the factor of luck, meaning conditions affecting the consequences of individual action which they could not reasonably be expected to foresee. (Luck is by no means wholly evil, as it is prominent in play and all free activity, and necessary to make activity interesting.) For reasons which cannot be developed here, but which should be fairly obvious, uncertainty and unpredictability play a tremendous and increasing role in individualistic organization, as the scale and intricacy of organization increase, as the interests of men center more in progress or getting ahead, and also as a consequence of a rising scale of living, which takes economic provision further and further away from the more elementary wants, which are fairly stable and predictable.

But the most important fact for the problem of freedom, in its aspect of effective freedom or a just distribution of power, is an inherent tendency of individualistic accumulation to proceed differentially, hence for inequality to increase cumulatively. Those who have more productive capacity at any time are obviously in a better position to save and invest, in themselves (knowledge, training) or in external wealth, and so to accumulate personal or physical capital and to increase their differential advantage over others. The situation suggests the scriptural saying, "To him that hath shall be given." But the importance of this cumulative tendency to increasing inequality is multiplied by the fact that it does not cease to operate at the end of the active life of the individual, but goes on from generation to generation. This is because the family, and not the individual, is from the long-run standpoint the real social unit. For what we call "individualism," "familism" would be a much more descriptive name. In this long view, again, the cumulative tendency is further distorted, and within limits intensified, by the role of uncertainty, the speculative character which economic life inevitably assumes in a society at once free, individualistic, or familistic, and progressive—i.e., where the maintenance and increase of the whole culture inheritance (material and immaterial, resources and wants) are left to the free action of individuals who also enjoy freedom in family life, including the freedom (even the duty) to make provision for their children. It is this situation which gives rise to relatively permanent inequality, the so-called "class structure" of society, and at least a tendency to its accentuation, in the absence of preventive measures.

To change the situation radically would call, as a beginning, for substantial abolition of the family as an institution. The difficulty in the way of such action is not merely that the family as such is considered sacrosanct, or the improbability of finding any workable substitute. It lies even more in the fact that freedom in family life is one of the essential freedoms desired by individuals themselves, and that this freedom, as desired and held sacred, includes the right (and duty) of parents to provide for their children, economically and culturally. Thus there is a profound contradiction between family freedom, or the rights of the individuals of one generation, and the right of the individuals of the succeeding generation to an equal start in life. In other words, there is a contradiction at the heart of the notion of equality or justice between free individuals, in that it involves rights which are inherently incompatible in the world as it is. For the individual is biologically an ephemeral unit; he comes into the world a liability and becomes an individual in the effective sense through sharing, via the family or some equivalent institution, in a culture inheritance (material and immaterial, power, knowledge, and taste) which is the product of social accumulation through the ages.

Moreover, abolition of inheritance through the family of the material or property factor in the culture accumulation—assuming that even that could be accomplished without functionally destroying the family—would be only a relatively short step toward the goal of equal or equitable distribution of opportunity among all individuals at birth. Something can, of course, be done along this line; and a great deal has, in fact, been done by the more advanced societies through drastic taxation of property inheritance, and of large incomes from whatever source derived, and the use of the proceeds to provide nonmaterial culture ("education") to the children of the poor and for the material relief of the indigent. The practical difficulties—political, economic, and social—of greatly extending action in this direction are very great, even if the public understood the problem and attacked it intelligently.

But space does not admit of carrying the investigation further—i.e., beyond the threshold of the problem. We can only hope that enough has been said to indicate the nature of the problem itself. It centers in the combination of the necessity of maintaining and increasing the total cultural inheritance, in which the material and immaterial factors, power and appreciation, are inseparable, with the ideal, also within limits a necessity, of effecting a distribution, as equitable as can be achieved, of this cultural inheritance, in its inseparable factors, among the individuals of each new generation as they come to adult life. Ethical individualism can only be realized or approached under the really unalterable conditions of human life on the earth, by social-political action, directed to making individuals what they "ought" to be, in their equipment with means and in the ends for which they wish to use the means under their control. As a social program, this situation obviously calls for depriving the private family of a very large part of its traditional functions, beginning with the most important of all, education in a very inclusive sense, and especially moral education, and transferring these to "society." This problem is not merely that of transferring the functions of the family to political units or jurisdictions as they now exist, culminating in the sovereign territorial state. In terms of any defensible general ideals, precisely the same problem arises in the relations between states, or between persons across state lines. The ultimate ideal would doubtless envision world humanity as an ideal family, an all-inclusive "brotherhood of man." But beyond the questions as to what that means, and as to the possibilities, it is also clear that no sharp boundary can be drawn around "humanity" itself, either on the side of inclusion or exclusion.

Such changes can only be effected very gradually at best, and only in the light of vastly more knowledge, and through more devotion than anyone now possesses, to say nothing of the great mass of the electorate, by whose action any change must come, if it is to be free action. But the first requirement, not yet achieved or in sight, if freedom is to be increased and life ennobled, is the creation, presumably by general education, of a disposition to attack the problems "rationally," in terms (a) of the facts of the situation and the possibilities of action and (b) reasonable clarity and agreement on the ideals to be achieved. In other words, the first step is to counteract the romanticism in social thinking, indeed the proliferation of varied and mutually antagonistic romanticisms—the cry for action without serious examination of its consequences, which seems to be the humanly natural way of acting, especially in a social crisis.

# V

# JUSTICE HOLMES: VOICE OF DEMOCRATIC EVOLUTION

## T. V. SMITH

❊

When the effervescence of democratic negation extends its working beyond the abolition of external distinctions of rank to spiritual things—when the passion for equality is not content with founding social intercourse upon universal human sympathy, and a community of interests in which all may share, but attacks the lines of Nature which establish orders and degrees among the souls of men—they are not only wrong, but ignobly wrong. Modesty and reverence are no less virtues of freemen than the democratic feeling which will submit neither to arrogance nor to servility.—HOLMES, "The Use of Law Schools" (in *Collected Legal Papers*).

THE paradox has frequently been remarked, and not infrequently observed, that democracy finds its most stalwart preservers among the aristocratic. In our own history, for instance, it was not Thomas Paine or Samuel Adams, the flaming revolutionaries, who preserved us democracy, but George Washington, aristocrat of the land, John Adams, aristocrat of the mind, and Thomas Jefferson, aristocrat of both. Not that the other type of patriotism had not and has not an indispensable role, but not the role of preserving. In our time no man has done more, I think, than Oliver Wendell Holmes, Jr., to safeguard democracy's future. Holmes, exponent equally in lineage and life of a pride and reserve truly royal, this is the latter-day aristocrat who has had both will and wit to articulate a stern but comprehensive

119

view of the universe with the practice of the democratic way of life. He is apostle of a discipline which alone can save democracy from the decadence of romanticism.

The explanation of the paradox, in Holmes once more illustrated, is simple enough at one level of thought. It is men who have a stake, who can be found when desired, who are not lacking in personal incentive to fight for their rights—these are the men upon whom enterprises of pith and moment depend. Traits which these illustrate—stability, prestige, honor—are ingredients of aristocracy under any definition of the term. The landed and the gifted are best able to preserve what they will, and they always have an adequate will to preserve a government which has honored their position with acceptance and which fairly promises to fulfil their expectations. That explanation, however, good as far as it goes, does not go far enough or deep enough: it is too simple to cover all the facts and too external to exhaust the spirit of the paradox that democracy relies upon aristocracy for survival.

#### I. HOLMES: DEMOCRACY'S MODEL ARISTOCRAT

There is another line of explanation to which it will pay us now to revert. I say "revert," for in the first chapter of this book I have set up a distinction in character between founders and preservers. The ones are primarily idea-men, the others primarily habit-men. Not that both do not have something of both, but each emphasizes his own. There is the revolutionary, like Thomas Paine, indispensable to the founding; and then there is the evolutionary, like George Washington, equally indispensable to the preserving of a democracy. Character counts for both, though different kinds of character; and honor, too, particularly the kind of honor essential to the mutuality which I shall develop at the end of this chapter. A society that can abide such incommensurables of character without making them incompatibles and so counting one of them in-

tolerable, such a society is democratic in genius and lacks only
instruments of achievement to become so in fact. It requires
only its voices to get the votes to keep it rolling.

"What form of government have you given us?" a citizen is
reported to have asked of Franklin as he came from the constitutional convention. "A republic," was his sage reply, but
with this caution characteristically attached, "if you can keep
it so!" It is the kind of character required to keep a republic
democratic which concerns us in this closing chapter.

Justice Oliver Wendell Holmes was our most aristocratic
voice to keep it so. The Holmes family, now run out like all
things too precious to endure, hailed from the Brahmins of
New England; and it covered, father and son together, almost
the entire span of our national life. Let me say a word upon
the peculiarly appropriate sounding board the son had, and
then analyze what it was he sounded forth so solvent for
democratic preservation.

The United States Supreme Court, to which Holmes came in
1902 after a distinguished career on the Massachusetts bench,
is the Areopagus of America. The Court is a philosophic institution, engaged exclusively upon interpretation, charting
through its semantic clairvoyance our national course in terms
of decades rather than of days or years. It is a moral body re-
affirming the copybook maxims of our constitutional yester-
days and determining which of them is the fit and proper tack
for a long line of tomorrows. It recognizes no sovereign save
its own discretion—its own discretion and God; and it itself
is the final interpreter of what God's will is for the nation. It
represents, as befits its philosophic nature, the most complete
divorce found on earth between the will-to-power and the
will-to-perfection, monopolizing as its own career our national will-to-perfection. It has no army, no navy, no air
force, no arsenal in reserve to enforce its decisions. It only
says what ought to be and leaves the "ought" to become the

"is" through techniques of power whose odium it in no sense shares. A position which philosophers have in every age dreamed of, from Plato down, but hardly expected to see realized on earth, was founded by our fathers and was promoted by the prowess of Marshall into sacrosanct eminence by a national dogma, our American doctrine of "judicial supremacy." Is there anybody else on earth who, incomparably secure of position, with social distance safeguarded and every normal want guaranteed, has only to ask himself this godlike thing: "What is the meaning of ancient words (Constitution), what the intent of modern words (the statute), and what the logical sequel of such semantic clairvoyance?" To ask such questions in security and to answer then in quietness—to make a career of this intellectual luxury is the vocation of a god. Yet this fair fortune has befallen the men who sit on the Olympian eminence of our Supreme Court.

Only a godlike man can grace such irresponsible eminence. Though all men are born equal, as the fathers phrased it, the sons have learned, in the words of a wit, that "fortunately some men get over it." Whoever with this supreme grace guaranteed does not outgrow equality with modesty will overgrow it with presumptuousness. Holmes outgrew equality and then like a true Olympian made it his career to accept its principle and to maintain its conditions. By "acceptance" I do not mean that Holmes put himself on a level with the generality; he was too honest an aristocrat not to recognize his own superiority. Impeccably as Holmes publicly maintains the egalitarian decorum expected in democracy, his aristocratic tastes come out unmistakably in his private letters, especially letters to his friend and peer, Sir Frederick Pollock. These tastes let us now sample, not to further the paradox but to explain how an aristocrat may serve democracy by making its conditions the major form of his *noblesse oblige*.

Writing to his fellow-Olympian, Holmes is at no pains, as I

say, to conceal his sense of superiority. "My aim below has been solely to make a few competents like you say that I had hit the *ut de poitrine* in my line."[1] Nor does he conceal disdain, albeit tolerant, for others: "How eternally amazed or amused one is at the convictions of one's neighbors—imperturbably admitting reciprocity."[2] And as for the generality of men, note this evaluation: "So far as my choice goes I would rather see a million fellahs go hungry . . . . than lose what we more or less have lost"[3] (he is speaking of the cultural treasures of Belgium, 1914). With a touch of disdain for the universal ignorance of simplicity and the simplicity of ignorance and the inadequacy of both, Holmes remarks that "one day's impact is better than a month of dead pull,"[4] and that "the only simplicity for which I would give a straw is that which is on the other side of the complex—not that which never has divined it."[5] "The greatest bores in the world are the come-outers who are cock-sure of a dozen nostrums."[6] This all but universal "frame of mind" among the vulgar, Holmes inelegantly admits, "makes me puke."[7]

On the positive side, Holmes's admiration was for men like James J. Hill, the railroad buccaneer, "representing one of the greatest forms of human power, an immense mastery of economic details, an equal grasp of general principles, and ability and courage to put his conclusions into practice with brilliant success when all the knowing ones said he would fail";[8] for measures like those on taxation proposed by the millionaire, Andrew W. Mellon, Secretary of the Treasury, which, though he thought Congress would turn them down, nevertheless, as he says, "seemed right to me";[9] for men like Darwin, who

---

[1] *Holmes-Pollock Letters* (2 vols.; Boston: Harvard University Press, 1941), II, 71

[2] *Ibid.*, II, 61.

[3] *Ibid.*, I, 221.

[4] *Ibid.*, I, 154.

[5] *Ibid.*, I, 109.

[6] *Ibid.*, II, 11.

[7] *Ibid.*, I, 235.

[8] *Ibid.*, I, 167.

[9] *Ibid.*, II, 137.

explained how the fittest survive, and than whom, observes Holmes, no other writer of English "has done so much to affect our whole way of thinking about the universe";[10] like Malthus, who shows how the unfitted perish, and who, as Holmes says, "a hundred years ago busted fallacies that politicians and labor leaders still live on";[11] for strenuous games like polo, in the "rough riding" of which, if once in a while "a neck is broken," Holmes regarded it "not as a waste, but as a price well paid for breeding of a race fit for leadership and command";[12] and for hard people like the Japanese, whom Holmes thought we would have to fight,[13] but whose "attitude, so far as I can picture it, on moral questions seems to me sounder than ours; with us morality tends to become a branch of Oxford exquisiteness. . . . . ."[14] Holmes quotes with evident approval a former Japanese student of his, Kaneko by name, to the effect that "the Japanese . . . . leave the next world to look out for itself and try to do their best in this . . . . they [have] the advantage of not being hampered by religion."[15]

Contrast with these admirations his distaste for philanthropies like those of Carnegie and Rockefeller, which, says he, "are *prima facie* the worst abuse of private ownership—from the economic point of view";[16] for measures like the Sherman Act to curb monopolies, which he brands as "humbug based on economic ignorance and incompetence";[17] for certain "gents," as he calls them, "who believe in the upward and onward rather more than I do";[18] and, in general, for the softheaded or tenderhearted like Bergson, Bertrand Russell, and even his old friend William James, each of whom, after praising as if for burial, Holmes then asphyxiates with a

[10] *Ibid.*, I, 58.          [11] *Ibid.*, I, 219.
[12] *Speeches* (Boston: Little, Brown & Co., 1934), p. 63.
[13] *Holmes-Pollock Letters*, II, 36.    [15] *Ibid.*, I, 97.      [17] *Ibid.*, I, 163.
[14] *Ibid.*, I, 100.          [16] *Ibid.*, I, 171.      [18] *Ibid.*, I, 201.

phrase: Bergson—"a humbug,"[19] "churning the void to make cheese";[20] Russell—"a sentimentalist . . . . does not talk well of war . . . . has a kind of respect for human criticism of or rebellion at the Cosmos, which to my mind is simply damning the weather, evidence that the speaker is ill-adjusted and not otherwise to be taken seriously";[21] James—"wishes led him to turn down the lights so as to give miracle a chance."[22]

If further evidence be needed of Holmes's membership in a sort of stern aristocracy, note (to Lady Pollock, 1898) his pleasure "in hearing some rattling jingo talk after the self-righteous and preaching discourse, which has prevailed to some extent at Harvard College and elsewhere."[23] And on the subject to which this remark leads, the subject of war, there is much to be said about Holmes, more than has yet been said. His friend Pollock wonders out loud in a letter, at what is hardly longer a matter of doubt, whether "that Antietam bullet didn't give you in its time some queer views of things in general."[24] Among views which some would regard queer, others perverse, are Holmes's notion that "the sacredness of human life is a purely municipal idea of no validity outside the jurisdiction," and his deep conviction—one of the few things about which he professes "no doubt"—"that every society rests on the death of men—as does also the romantic interest of long established lands."[25] As fine a symbol as one might conceive of this hard aristocratic temperament sitting upon Olympus and functioning in the unhurried perspective of the ages is found in Holmes's habit, frequently remarked by him and not always without a tinge of the boastful, of ignoring passing events. "I don't read the papers or otherwise feel the pulse of the machine. I merely speculate."[26]

---

[19] *Ibid.*, I, 217.

[20] *Ibid.*, II, 75.

[21] *Ibid.*, II, 158.

[22] *Ibid.*, I, 167.

[23] *Ibid.*, I, 87.

[24] *Ibid.*, I, 150.

[25] *Ibid.*, II, 36.

[26] *Ibid.*, I, 124.

And what, may we now ask, does an aristocrat in democratic times speculate about, an aristocrat who graces such transcendence as the Supreme Court while the races of men go by? What social employments does he find for his great talents? Well, strange as it may sound, Holmes made it his business responsibly to speculate on how to maintain and prosper a system "conceived in liberty and dedicated to the proposition that all men are created equal." This paradox of equalitarianism our aristocrat accepted with independent piety as he accepted the paradox of intermittent war for purposes of peace and progress.

But before detailing the specific form of this acceptance on his part, with especial reference to the philosophy of democracy precipitated thereby, let us remind ourselves why it is important for democrats to understand a man like Holmes. It is important, first, because there are a lot of such men, who, though as tories they may be coerced into acquiescence during revolutionary times, must as citizens be assimilated for the long, evolutionary pull. Democracy cannot simply liquidate its lords. It is important, second, because they represent visibly what is covert in every humblest democrat, the egoistic, the prideful—yes, the aspirational side of every son of man. In short, and finally, such aristocrats do but personalize the aristocratic and dynamic daydreams of all the units of democracy itself.

## II. HOLMES'S PHILOSOPHY OF DEMOCRACY

Rumor had it that Holmes, Second Lieutenant Holmes, was caught reading the *Leviathan* of old Thomas Hobbes when notified of his promotion to a first lieutenancy in the Civil War. The rumor is most apt, not merely in the perview of Hobbes's hard-boiled philosophy, but in the general perspective of Holmes's entire life. Hobbes he knew at perhaps eighteen, but Locke he admitted he had not read even at eighty!

The contrast is crucial. Hobbes is driven to desperate conclusions of a totalitarian nature by the strenuous premises from which he starts. These premises about man Holmes shares with Hobbes, the chief of which is man's antisocial curse and the conflicts of interest necessitated as consequence thereof. "I do think," said he at seventy-nine, "that man at present is a predatory animal."[27] The phrase "at present" signifies only the caution of everlasting open-mindedness in Holmes; it does not limit his belief in the inevitability of conflict. And yet that belief is limited; it is limited slightly by the occasional occurrence of spiritual saints and by secular aristocrats who have the moral equivalent of saintliness in their devoted quest of the perfect word, the perfect deed, the symmetrical self developed to the top of its potentiality. These, however, are the rare exception and in no sense the rule. After remarking this exception in his famous address upon accepting a doctorate from Yale University, in 1886, Holmes turns aside to reaffirm for the generality his old belief that "most men do and must reach the same result under the illusion of self-seeking."[28] This all but universal self-seeking is "illusory" not to men themselves but to aristocrats like Holmes, who see what men do not see—namely, that "the crowd if it knew more wouldn't want what it does."[29] That "if," however, is, as Holmes admits, strictly "immaterial," because downright contrary to fact. The fact is, and it is a bottom fact to Holmes as to Hobbes, that men are irremediably and inexorably in conflict with one another.

Given such conflicts, resulting from man's predatory nature, we must have either dictatorship, with its suppression of adverse talents, or democracy, with legislative leeways which sound like the elevation of loud noise and look like the licens-

[27] *Ibid.*, II, 36.
[28] *Collected Legal Papers* (New York: Harcourt, Brace & Co., 1920), p. 34.
[29] *Holmes-Pollock Letters*, I, 163.

ing of mediocrity. Had Holmes arisen under dictatorship, he *could* have abided it better than most, for he had meat to eat that dictators know not of; and he probably *would* have abided it, for he was no revolutionary. But he was born and nurtured under brighter stars—so he made the most of democracy; for, I repeat, Holmes was no revolutionary. In democratic times he had the genius to discern, as most do not, and the stamina to accept spiritually, as most sensitive souls cannot, the conditions required for such a society. These conditions were realized in him as: (1) *cosmic modesty combined with personal pride;* (2) *political tolerance to the nethermost limit;* then (3) *nationally and internationally, war to the hilt against the bellicose intolerant;* but (4) in the meantime, *the allowance municipally of leeway for the legislative to function foolishly if it must be, wisely if it may be.* Let us now dilate upon Holmes's philosophy of democracy around this formulation of its conditions, taking them up in reverse order.

LEEWAY FOR THE LEGISLATIVE

At its best the legislative process is hard to tolerate and at its worst it is almost impossible to stomach. Its obvious noise and its apparent inefficiency offend even the humblest who survey its work from congressional galleries. Showmanship tends to supplant statesmanship, and, harder to bear, exhibitionism seems to become the personal propaedeutic to that interchange called "lathering one another's ego." Considering how this appears to us ordinary people, imagine how it would strike aristocratic tastes like those of Holmes. And, if you would see the full measure of his aristocratic tolerance, you must add one other count—a count that judges less aristocratic than he often presumed upon adversely—the accepted doctrine of the supremacy of the judicial. It has long been respectable (many would say "dutiful") for Supreme Court justices, whatever their rationalization of it, to presume upon their preferred position to keep the legislative branch of our government in its place—a place secondary if not tertiary. When the respect-able—and, if you will, the dutiful—jibe with the personally and the professionally prideful, the temptation to little men becomes irresistible.

Holmes, whatever else one may say of him, was not a little man. Magnanimity is the grace which best becomes an aristo-crat. At the level of statesmanship this trait takes the form of *noblesse oblige* toward the legislative method of evolutionary progress. Holmes's attitude as a judge toward the legislative is impeccably magnanimous. His attitude is as impeccable in deed as in word, and all the world knows his words against judges who read their own predilections into law under cover of constitutionalism. His articulation of such right of way for the legislative took both the negative and the positive form, and in both forms not only went the limit, but also extended the limit.

On the negative side, Holmes thought that judges ought to abstain from utilizing the influence which respectability granted them, that of overriding legislative enactments on grounds of policy. The legislature is the policy-forming branch of government, and must be so in a democratic society. If it became necessary to resort to devices diabolical to outwit one's own nefarious temperament, then the judge ought to pay that price. It was this larger point which Holmes had in mind in declaring that judges, who as he says are "apt to be naif, simple-minded men," "need something of Mephistopheles . . . . to learn to transcend our own convictions and to leave room for much that we hold dear to be done away with short of revolution by the orderly change of law."[30] He went so far in his roominess as to admit that he did not think the nation would end if judges lost their power to declare any national legislation void.[31] That is the final act of judicial abnegation. It has little to do with this point, though much to do with the

[30] *Collected Legal Papers*, p. 295.          [31] *Ibid.*, pp. 295–96.

philosophy of federalism, for Holmes to add to that abnegation that the "Union would be imperilled if we could not make that declaration as to the laws of the several States."[32]

Positively, Holmes thought that the people had the right to determine their own policy—and that meant legislative leeway to do through their direct representatives what they wanted to do at any given time. It is not the business of the judiciary to determine policy, not even under cover, but only to keep policies from being downright inhuman and to make them at any given time consistent throughout the nation and across the gulf of time that separates one generation from another. This right of the people includes the privilege of their making fools of themselves. About that Holmes was absolutely certain, and the result, however deplorable to the private conscience of an aristocrat, was strictly immaterial to public policy in a democracy. The fact was to him not only logically immaterial but personably tolerable because normally expected. Upon the positive conviction that the Constitution had planned a democracy which would be always on the grow, Holmes was always disposed to bend the Constitution to what the people wanted rather than to what he personally thought wise.

It is most probable that Holmes's temperament would have always made him, as a man, inimical to popular legislation. His personal distaste is on record for much that passed for popular in his day, and he went out on a wave of New Dealism with little of which I believe he sympathized. It is certain, whatever his temperament, that another logic, one available and one practiced by judicial contemporaries, would have justified his preferences to sit upon the legislative when it was helping the people make fools of themselves. Holmes, however, whether in the minority or the majority, persisted in his

[32] *Ibid.*, p. 296.

allowance of autonomy for the legislative and of leeway in the exercise of that autonomy.

It is just here that there comes best to the surface the difference between such a revolutionary as Thomas Paine and such an evolutionary as Oliver Wendell Holmes. To identify natural rights with what is *right* is to be a revolutionary, if one have then for action the courage of his conscience. This is to emancipate ideas from actualities and let them float free, following in their lovely train. Useful against outsiders, this moralizing of putative rights is suicidal if applied too strictly to insiders; for it makes it impossible for the legislative to function through its genius of give and take. Grand as a revolutionary, Paine would have been a flop as an evolutionary—i.e., a legislator.

Holmes, however, though perhaps a little elegant for the arena, would in spirit have been as good a legislator as he was a judge. Unlike the revolutionary idea-men, Holmes never emancipated ideas from their implementation to pursue them into thin air. He does not identify natural rights with *the right;* or, in so far as he allows this popular identification, he then brushes the right itself away as immaterial to law. This is the context in which Holmes declares that he would "be glad if we could get rid of the whole moral phraseology which . . . . has tended to distort the law,"[33] and the context in which he advises that we had best conceive the law not as good men regard it but as "our friend the bad man" conceives it—i.e., "prophecies of what the courts will do in fact. . . . ."[34]

Generalizing this conviction into a philosophy, Holmes declares that "manifestly nothing but confusion of thought can result from assuming that the rights of man in a moral sense are equally rights in the sense of the Constitution and the law."[35] This is the prudent rhetoric of compromise, of the

[33] *Holmes-Pollock Letters*, II, 200.
[34] *Collected Legal Papers*, p. 173.
[35] *Ibid.*, p. 172.

Founding Fathers. Men may have a thousand private fancies of perfection; they may even be willing to fight for them; and, if they fight, they might indeed win. That is all well and good; it is revolution, and revolution has its place in the drama of fate. But revolution ends with what further evolution must begin with, conflicting ideas of what the right is, and it issues—if issue it does—into a determination of what is right. "The law," as Holmes ardently believes with Hobbes, "the law is the public conscience."[36] Whoever cannot accept this "public conscience," constituted through compromise, as superior for collective action to his own private conscience, however constituted, is not good timber for democratic evolution, however heroic he may have been in founding democracy. They also serve democracy heroically who only sit and compromise. "I say to you in all sadness of conviction," admonishes Holmes, "that to think great thoughts you must be heroes as well as idealists."[37]

In a conflict of interests where God alone knows what's right, and where God does not tell, or tells too many men differently, it becomes more important to settle the issue than it is to settle it "right." The actual settlement, if accepted in good faith, becomes for that situation the only "right" which men can realize. It is in the light of this principle, a principle more creative than the revolutionary can allow, that Holmes summarizes his philosophy of both judicial abstention and legislative leeway. It is, as he says,

precisely because I believe that the world would be just as well off if it lived under laws that differed from ours in many ways, and because I believe that the claim of our especial code to respect is simply that it exists, that it is the one to which we have become accustomed and not that it represents an eternal principle, I am slow to consent to overruling a precedent, and think that our important duty is to see that the judicial duel shall be fought out in the accustomed way.[38]

[36] *Leviathan* ("Everyman" ed.; New York: E. P. Dutton & Co., 1928), p. 172.
[37] *Collected Legal Papers*, p. 32.          [38] *Ibid.*, p. 239.

WAR FOR THE GORDIAN KNOTS OF LIFE

All this forbearance for the legislative determination of social policy arose not from sentimentalism but from acceptance of a very hard fact. That fact was and is that when reasonable consultation breaks down, war is man's only recourse. The choice is between evils, but is not for that reason avoidable. Legislation is bad, loose-jointed in operation, and mediocre in output, but it is not so wasteful as war. War is bad, very bad, but not itself the worst that can befall man. Holmes's attitude toward war seems clear, even if ambivalent. He hated it, as he is at pains to repeat. As a young captain, at home recovering from Civil War wounds all but mortal, he shocked the young ladies, he says, by declaring, what he ever believed, that "war is an organized bore";[39] and when old he admitted to Pollock that the survival value which he emphasized is in the case of war diseugenic. Yet Holmes regarded war as a personal discipline of value and not without its beneficent effects on civilization. This was the one side of his ambivalence.

The other side was that even if war were wholly evil, Holmes yet saw no way to avoid its necessity. If men will not compromise conflicting claims, even when conscientiously sacrosanct—that is what legislatures are tolerated for—then they must fight about them, until somebody stoops to compromise or somebody dies. We may here remark Holmes's conviction, expressed to Pollock, "that force mitigated so far as may be by good manners, is the *ultima ratio*, and between two groups that want to make inconsistent kinds of world I see no remedy except force."[40] Holmes had in mind precisely the kind of otherwise irremediable conflict upon which the world is now engaged, even to the point of clairvoyance of this very conflict; for he proceeds in this same context against Pollock's high hope for the League of Nations, "I find it somewhat hard to believe that we can come to such intimate understanding with the East that future slaughter can be avoided."[41] After a

[39] *Holmes-Pollock Letters*, II, 36.        [40] *Ibid.*        [41] *Ibid.*

general comparing of notes with Pollock on the subject of
pacifism, Holmes writes: "I agree with your condemnation of
armchair pacifists on the general ground that until the world
has got farther along war not only is not absurd but is inevitable and rational—though," as he adds in the spirit of his
honest ambivalence, "of course I would make great sacrifices
to avoid one."[42]

Let us now summarize these two characteristics of Holmes's
philosophy, preparatory to a discussion of the other two.
Conflicts are inevitable between men, for men are far from fully
socialized. The pressure of population—which Holmes after
Darwin and Malthus puts great stress upon—is a constant recurring cause in the grand manner of conflicts that will not be
settled peacefully. Gains made by sublimating that pressure in
forms of justice will only be, as he opines to Pollock, "expended at once in more population."[43] Conflicts arising from
this and other sources are not only inevitable but are often
irremediable. War, or the equivalent of war, results. One ac-
cepts this result with natural piety. "I don't pass moral judgments, least of all on nations. I see the inevitable everywhere."[44]

Holmes sees a germ of reason, indeed, in this hard way of
war, not merely because it must be accepted by all as inevitable
but also because he had a livelier sense than most of the continuity of this stern process and the milder processes represented in argument, in legislation, and even in adjudication.
Legislation in particular is a sort of domestic war, in which,
as he puts it in his "Ideals and Doubts," we only "shift disagreeable burdens from the shoulders of the stronger to those
of the weaker."[45] Courts are the projections into social policy
of the predilections of judges—he refers to their function as the
maintaining of the "judicial duel"—[46]and all social life is a

[42] *Ibid.*, II, 230.    [44] *Ibid.*, II, 230.

[43] *Ibid.*, II, 47.    [45] *Collected Legal Papers*, p. 305.    [46] *Ibid.*, p. 239.

sort of sublimated battle, in which prowess and pressure count for more than sentimentalists can allow or rationalists believe. "As law embodies beliefs that have triumphed in the battle of ideas and then have translated themselves into action, while there still is doubt, while opposite convictions still keep a battle front against each other, the time for law has not come, the notion destined to prevail is not yet entitled to the field."[47] This will but recall to the knowing, in fashion subdued, Holmes's more youthful declaration in the grand manner that "truth is the majority vote of that nation that could lick all others."[48] This keen Darwinian sense of continuity, which deserves extended comment, drives Holmes to a judgment that the difference between war and peace is a matter of degree rather than of kind. If one is rational, then rational is the other, in varying degree. Perhaps we can put his thought finally in this fair manner: war is the *ultima facie* of reason, legislation and adjudication the *prima facie* of reason.

### TOLERATION FOR ONLY THE TOLERABLE

As, however, the relatively low degree of rationality and the lower degree of desirability in war drive Holmes, politically, to allow autonomy for the legislative as sublimatory of the martial, so they drive him, socially, to proclaim tolerance to the nethermost limit of national survival. Not only for our friends and their ideas which we approve, not only for our enemies and their ideas which we loath, but also for enemies of our country up to the far point where their liberty of expression is analogous to the license of yelling "fire" in a crowded theater. Short of this long limit, Holmes believed in the positive beneficence of all such freedom. He did not doubt that talk is mostly nonsense, but it pleases men to make it; so who was he to interrupt the hedonic flow of their laryngeal liquidity? That is what life is mostly about—to revel in its own

[47] *Ibid.*, pp. 294–95.  [48] *Ibid.*, p. 310.

functioning at whatever level it does function. Holmes writes
to Pollock in connection with his having become the scape-
goat in the Court's decision in the Debs case: "It is one of the
ironies that I, who probably take the extremest view in favor
of free speech (in which, in the abstract, I have no enthusiastic
belief, though I hope I would die for it), that I should have
been selected for blowing up."[49]

But, turning to the most constructive side of Holmes's doctrine of tolerance, there is a "platitude" which once came to
him with what he calls "quasi religious force." It was that
"life is an end in itself. Functioning is all there is."[50] Veritably this insight, which is far from a platitude to many, became
for Holmes a genuine substitute for religion. It drove him, as
he confessed to Pollock, to take "the side of the unregenerate
who affirm the worth of life as an end in itself as against the
saints who deny it."[51] It permitted him the moral latitude to
declare that "it would be well if the intelligent classes could
forget the word sin and think less of being good,"[52] and also
to generalize, as already indicated, that it would be better for
the law "if we could get rid of the whole moral phraseology
which has tended to distort the law."[53] He speaks here of the
"intelligent," but in connection with freedom of speech it is
difficult to tell who the intelligent are. Nature has distributed
very widely the ability to talk—hardly any simian "functioning" is more steady, more conspicuous, or more self-satisfying
than is the laryngeal. The fool is just as much cheated out of
the meaning of his life when not allowed to spout his foolishness to those foolish enough to like to listen as the wise man is

[49] *Holmes-Pollock Letters*, II, 28–29.

[50] *Ibid.*, II, 22.                    [51] *Ibid.*, I, 101.

[52] *Ibid.*, II, 178. On his aristocratic "consciousness of kind," cf. his remark earlier
at a Harvard Law School dinner that "when the ignorant are taught to doubt they do
not know what they safely may believe" (*Collected Legal Papers*, p. 292).

[53] *Holmes-Pollock Letters*, II, 200.

when not allowed to share his wisdom with tastes equally precious. The distinction itself is hard to maintain on the aristocratic plane, whose *noblesse oblige* Holmes once wryly formulated to Pollock in this phrase: "We all are kind to those who think us great men."[54] It takes intelligence to appreciate intelligence; and, conversely, those who appreciate greatness must themselves be somehow great. The difficulty of the distinction between wisdom and foolishness grows harder still when we observe universally that nobody classifies himself seriously as a fool. The price which self-acknowledged wisdom pays for its laryngeal right of way is permission for what it calls foolishness to disport itself. It is not too great a price, especially since no one has to listen or personally abide everyone. It is not a penalty, anyhow, even when it is a heavy price; for it affords the privilege to wisdom not only to display itself but also to demonstrate its superiority.

Tolerance, then, is justified of both its direct and its indirect fruits. Indirectly it smuggles one himself in under the leeway which he allows others. Directly it permits each to experiment with the type of "functioning" out of which he can get the maximum fun. Holmes attaches two streamers to the aureole with which he graces the "quasi religious platitude" to which we have already referred. The first is that "our [at least his and Pollock's!] keenest pleasure is in what we call the higher sort."[55] This constitutes, however, no absolute warrant to elevate self or to depreciate others, for in a wider perspective Holmes at once expresses the wonder whether "cosmically an idea is any more important than the bowels."[56] So whether the functioning be cerebral or intestinal, it is worth while in itself and of whatever exterior worth others find it to be. Others cannot find anything concerning it, however, unless they permit it. Intrinsically and extrinsically, therefore, tolerance is indicated, lest men themselves make greater still

[54] *Ibid.*, I, 169.          [55] *Ibid.*, II, 22.          [56] *Ibid.*, II, 22.

the already greatest cosmic tragedy—a thought to which
Holmes often recurs—the "anguish," not of dying, but of
dying before one has had his "opportunity,"[57] before one has
"tested out his powers"[58]—in short, before one has enjoyed
the fulfilling of his "function."[59] To swell with human deeds
the cosmic woe is to wrong the universe as well as to defraud
man of what he might indeed enjoy. Since, as Holmes says,
"Life is like an artichoke; each day, week, month, year, gives
you one little bit which you nibble off—but precious little
compared to what you throw away,"[60] it becomes man as a
"cosmic ganglion" to conserve all that is offered. Tolerance is
man's way of co-operating with a niggard-enough Nature to
minimize mortal woes and to maximize all human joys.

### COSMIC MODESTY WITH PERSONAL PRIDE

It would, therefore, take a wiser man than Holmes claimed
himself to be not to allow up to the maximum limit freedom of
speech. The tolerance of Holmes rests at bottom upon his
modesty. All philosophy comes back at last, whether admitted or not, to something personal. Holmes had the grace
to admit the personal thing from which in his case all things
issue, to which all things return. Intellectually it was agnos-
ticism, emotionally it was modesty; in his own neat words it
was "the great act of faith" involved in the decision that he
himself was "not God."[61]

Such a decision is necessary if democracy is not to skid from
leadership into the *führer-princip*. "When you know that you
know," Holmes writes to his friend Pollock, "persecution
comes easy. It is as well that some of us don't know that we
know anything."[62] Earlier he had written in a decision for all
men to see that "persecution for the expression of opinion

---

[57] *Ibid.*, I, 29.                  [60] *Ibid.*, I, 30.
[58] *Ibid.*                           [61] *Collected Legal Papers*, p. 304.
[59] *Ibid.*                           [62] *Holmes-Pollock Letters*, II, 253.

seems perfectly logical. If you have no doubt of your premises or your power and want a certain result with all your heart you . . . . naturally sweep away all opposition."[63] To Holmes, truth, as he said over and over again, was merely what he could not help believing; and whether there was a "truth of truth," as he put it, he admitted that he did not and could not know.[64] Nor did he know whether there is a "can't help" for the universe.

The tolerance to which this cosmic modesty gave birth was not the mere sufferance of disdain. The test of tolerance is not what we approve but what we loathe. Such modesty not only makes a man a good neighbor, but it is this spirit which reaches out far beyond the we-group orbit and explains Justice Holmes's attitude toward his governmental competitor, the legislature. In discussing heretofore the leeway which he philosophically allowed legislation we did not get quite to the bottom of the matter. Here is the bottom—a personal incapacity to play the role of deity and so a personal unwillingness to get along without the constructive aid of fellow-men in determining what is true and just. Holmes makes this larger matter clear in allowing the Sherman Act to function, when he disapproved it, and the Interstate Commerce Commission to fix rates, when he doubted it "a fit body to be entrusted with rate-making, even in the qualified way it is entrusted."[65] But this whole confession of no faith in his own omniscience will bear quoting: "Of course," he writes Pollock, "I enforce whatever constitutional laws Congress or anybody else sees fit to pass—and do it in good faith to the best of my ability. . . . . I am so sceptical as to our knowledge about the goodness or badness of laws that I have no practical criticism [criterion?] except what the crowd wants. Personally I bet that the crowd if it knew more wouldn't want what it does—but that is immaterial."[66] "The chief end of man," Holmes liked to say as if in

[63] *Ibid.*      [64] *Ibid.*      [65] *Ibid.*, I, 163.      [66] *Ibid.*

correction of the ancient creed, "is to form general propositions"—adding that "no general proposition is worth a
damn."[67]

In this recurring confession of ignorance, there seems lacking in Holmes the spirit of irony always present in Socrates.
Holmes was sincere: he really knew that he didn't know.
From his sincere ignorance there grew magnanimity and there
flowed tolerance for all varieties of men, acceptance of legislation as man's most fruitful method of collective progress, and
proclamation of the way of war when tolerance meets its
nemesis in those made intolerant by their lack of just this
democratic modesty. This conscious cosmic ignorance is the
larger key to Holmes's social tolerance.

What I have been describing as cosmic modesty, first fruit
of admitted ignorance, is not, however, what passes for humility. No man was ever further from being humble than
Holmes. "If I haven't done my share," said he to his fellow-
aristocrat, Pollock—whose good opinion he always craved—
"in the way of putting in new and remodeling old thought for
the last twenty years then I delude myself."[68] Holmes lived
and reveled in what he himself impersonally describes as

the secret joy of the thinker, who knows that, a hundred years after
he is dead and forgotten, men who never heard of him will be moving to the measure of his thought—the subtle rapture of a postponed
power, which the world knows not because it has no external trap-
pings, but which to his prophetic vision is more real than that which
commands an army."[69]

Humility is a Christian virtue, being pride slightly touched
at the fringe with the pathological. Holmes was a Stoic, an
ancient Stoic born out of time, but with pride undisguised and
unashamed. He lacked humility as much as he possessed modesty; he lacked humanitarianism as much as he possessed solic-

[67] *Ibid.*, II, 14.     [68] *Ibid.*, I, 106.     [69] *Collected Legal Papers*, p. 32.

itude for the human race. I began by saying that Holmes was an aristocrat. Now I must end by showing how his type of cosmic modesty, accompanied by personal pride, can transform democracy into an aristocracy for every citizen. Holmes himself equates the two in declaring that "modesty and reverence are no less virtues of freemen than the democratic feeling which will submit neither to arrogance nor servility."[70]

### III. THE ARISTOCRACY OF DEMOCRACY

There is really no deep incompatibility between aristocracy and democracy; the latter is but the principle of the former generalized. The compatibility between them is, however, a little too deep for all who run to see. Indeed, it requires the glasses of civilization to discern what civilization requires. To Pollock, who had remarked the impairment of justice by ignorance, Holmes replies: "You speak for the need of a certain modicum of intelligence for justice. It seems to me that the whole scheme of salvation depends on having a required modicum of intelligence."[71] And already in a famous speech Holmes had declared to the same end, but more generally, that "for most of the things that properly can be called evils . . . . the main remedy . . . . is for us to grow more civilized."[72] It is a large order, as Professor Knight has shown above, and yet an order without which there is little hope for the human race. We must see in general, as Knight has made apparent with regard to liberty, what is involved in becoming more civilized, so that we may discern how democracy, which has to-day more than ever become civilization's synonym, fulfils the vision of an aristocratic world.

To Holmes civilization meant two great things: the lesser one external, the greater internal. The external condition of civilization is peace. I speak of peace as a "condition," for

[70] *Ibid.*, p. 38.

[71] *Holmes-Pollock Letters*, II, 178.          [72] *Collected Legal Papers*, p. 296.

Holmes saw how far it is from being an end in itself. As against what he called "the barbaric thirst of conquest,"[73] there are the sublimating processes of peace. We have already observed that peaceful sublimation of war differs from war only in degree. We may have even intimated that the degree for Holmes is small. So the difference between men and women is little; but, as the wag remarked relievedly, "Thank God for that little!" "Beyond the vision of battling races and an impoverished earth," says Holmes with unwonted eloquence, "I catch a dreaming glimpse of peace."[74] Holmes differed from most not in not desiring peace but in seeing that its price is so great, and indeed so much like war, that few can make the desire for it come true. Domestic peace requires civilized self-control, and international peace requires, as Holmes never doubted, population control as well as a growing tolerance. Now nothing is more difficult than tolerance, and few things are so easy and delightful, as he was wont wryly to remark to Chief Justice White, his Catholic colleague, as replenishing the population.[75] Dilating upon the difficulties of peace, Holmes saw as a lawyer that all legislation is a battle; he saw as a judge that all adjudication is but a respite in man's everlasting struggle for advantage, a respite in which what the judge takes to be "first principles are believed by half his fellow men to be wrong."[76] But what makes all this bad, makes its only alternative, war, worse.

So the external thing which civilization demands is that men accept the morally and aesthetically mediocre as the rule of collective life. To demand more than can be got through democratic compromise is to get less than the compromise itself would yield. Half a loaf is still more than no bread at all, and much more than the bread for most that comes from war over wheat. To accept the game of compromise and to play it

[73] *Ibid.*, p. 31.                [75] *Holmes-Pollock Letters*, II, 41.

[74] *Ibid.*, p. 297.                [76] *Collected Legal Papers*, p. 295.

according to the rules prevailing, "whether I like them or not,"[77] this is the first mark of a civilized man. It represents a great concession—indeed, recession from the standards of perfection which every humblest man carries around with him privately. But public life is not a private show—it is anybody's and everybody's chance to better himself, and in it one will do worse than the mediocre who demands a better than the best that can be achieved through the processes of give and take.

It is the fact that Holmes sees man's collective life so external and inferior a thing that he makes little of those who try to make too much of it. If a man asks you for your coat, give him your cloak also; for what is cloth compared to the skin lost in fighting him for it? Against socialism, for instance, which was to Holmes the easy example of the overestimation of that form of the external called economic, he has many words—words sometimes more winged than weighty perhaps. Marxism's would-be scientific statistics Holmes damns as "sentimental and dramatic economics."[78] His apparent objection to socialism is that no form of reallocating the external will work satisfactorily for all, or for long; but his real objection is that socialists find the meaning of life in the external, or, if in the internal, an internal grown aggressive through envy. To achieve the good life is easier without external goods than with them if they substitute for internal fineness and stamina. Speaking of the Webbs and others who sought justice through more equal distribution of economic opportunity, Holmes inquires:

What do the luxuries of the few really amount to? I believe them to be a drop in the bucket. The luxuries that really impinge upon the necessaries are the luxuries of the many, e.g., the Churches. And if you abolished them, do you doubt that the addition would be expended at once in more population? I don't.[79]

[77] *Ibid.*, p. 307.       [78] *Holmes-Pollock Letters*, II, 47.       [79] *Ibid.*, II, 29.

This, indeed, is one thing which so devout a disciple of Malthus as Holmes was would hardly think of doubting. Pursuing the same point constructively and in criticism of certain Americans who overemphasized the economic, Holmes declares:

Beard I thought years ago when I read him went into rather ignoble though painstaking investigations of the investments of the leaders, with an innuendo even if disclaimed. I shall believe until compelled[80] to think otherwise that they wanted to make a nation and invested (bet)[81] on the belief that they would make one, not that they wanted a powerful government because they had invested. Belittling arguments always have a force of their own, but you and I believe that high-mindedness is not impossible to man.[82]

Holmes's distrust of socialism extended to every external effort at human amelioration. He had "no belief in panaceas and almost none in sudden ruin."[83] As against what comes to man from without, Holmes put what happens to man within —the cultural, the imaginative,[84] the internal. All things good come gradually (how gradually!)—as slowly as self-knowledge and self-control. Beginning with a rich cultural inheritance, the civilized man will continue until he has elaborated out of living experience a personal philosophy in which man's life shades off into a cosmic life whose reach into immensity gives to man's littleness its final greatness.

This was to Holmes a very deep and far-reaching conviction. It distinguished philosophy from gossip[85] and left him such

[80] Note his ever recurring open-mindedness. In matters even more cosmic and important he tells Pollock: "I am far from believing with them [Eddington *et al.*], but I am entirely ready to believe it on proof" (*ibid.*, II, 252).

[81] "As to the universe my formula as a betalitarian (one who thinks you can bet about but not know), is a spontaneity taking an irrational pleasure in a moment of rational sequence" (*ibid.*, II, 22).

[82] *Ibid.*, II, 222–23.                    [83] *Collected Legal Papers*, p. 295.

[84] "For lack of imagination, five dollars" (*ibid.*, p. 201).

[85] *Ibid.*, pp. 159, 166.

philosophy as was a personal religion. "As life draws near the end . . . . I think rather more than ever that man has respected himself too much and the universe too little. He has thought of himself as a god and has despised 'brute matter,' instead of thinking his importance to be all of a piece with the rest."[86] This conviction betokens no recession of what I have been calling personal pride, but an extension of the person so that pride in it can become respect for a cosmic enterprise—can become, in short, natural piety. He who has such pride has his back against the wall of the universe; he can enjoy himself with safe abandon and can fight, if fight he must, with unbeatable morale. Over and over to Pollock, his safe friend, Holmes describes man as a "cosmic ganglion," but he cautions his young and new-found Chinese friend, Wu, to treat this confession of faith as of too personal and private a nature for repetition.[87] He profoundly dislikes men who "employ the energy that is furnished to us by the cosmos to defy it and shake our fist at the sky. It seems to me silly."[88]

In lesser men this pride, which becomes natural piety for whatever is and ends in reverence for all that is, in lesser men, I say, this attitude might have turned into something sectarian, as in Holmes's fellow-Bostonian, Borden P. Bowne, the personalist. In less self-reliant men it might have turned into theism and produced men who, as Holmes dramatically puts it, cannot respect the universe unless it "wears a beard."[89] In mere moderns, so newly emancipated as not yet to be civilized, it would have become just pantheism. Holmes was no sectarian and not merely a modern; he was, as I have said, a Stoic belatedly appearing in modern times. As a modern it became his lot to articulate biological continuity as with Darwin and metaphysical continuity as with Spinoza with the emotional continuity, the natural piety, of the ancient who

[86] *Holmes-Pollock Letters*, II, 234.
[87] *Book Notices, etc.*, p. 165.
[88] *Collected Legal Papers*, p. 315.
[89] *Holmes-Pollock Letters*, I, 161.

could exclaim: "No longer Dear City of Cecrops, but now Dear City of God."

Such a view of the world turned Holmes away from all idealistic philosophies as sentimentalisms and toward all materialistic views which retained for themselves the wonder and reverence which the older Lucretius had. At a time when idealism was rampant among technical philosophers, Holmes sided with Brooks Adams, who had told him that "the philosophers were hired by the comfortable class to prove that everything is all right." Holmes, commenting on this, says: "I think it *is* all right, but on very different grounds."[90] He admired the modern philosophers who caught these grounds without jumping the ground altogether: Santayana, who, as he says, "comes nearer to me than most philosophers";[91] Dewey, of whose book, *Experience and Nature*, Holmes writes,

although incredibly ill written, it seemed to me after several readings to have a feeling of intimacy with the inside of the cosmos that I found unequaled. So methought God would have spoken had he been inarticulate but keenly desirous to tell you how it was."[92]

This is central and crucial to Holmes, this conception of an integrated world of which the self is an organic part. In his searching address upon "The Profession of the Law," he says:

To those who believe with me that not the least godlike of man's activities is the large survey of causes . . . . I say . . . . that a man may live greatly in the law as well as elsewhere; that there as well as elsewhere his thought may find its unity in an infinite perspective. . . . . All that life offers any man from which to start his thinking is a fact. And if this universe is one universe, if it is so far thinkable that you can pass in reason from one part of it to another, it does not matter very much what that fact is. For every fact leads to every other by the path of the air. Only men do not yet see how, always. And your business as thinkers is to make plainer the way from

[90] *Ibid.*, I, 139.

[91] *Book Notices, etc.*, p. 169.          [92] *Holmes-Pollock Letters*, II, 287.

some thing to the whole of things; to show the rational connection between your fact and the frame of the universe.[93]

Again he says, in the same address:

No man has earned the right to intellectual ambition until he has learned to lay his course by a star which he has never seen. . . . .[94]

And finally, from the vocation of law he passes as is his wont to the whole vocation of life:

The mark of a master is, that facts which before lay scattered in an inorganic mass, when he shoots through them the magnetic current of his thought, leap into an organic order, and live and bear fruit.[95]

Doubt, wonder, tolerance—this is the trinity with which Holmes would transform externalism into a cosmic-centered life. His pantheistic attitude toward the universe prevented this philosophy from becoming a pathological introversion and his toughness of fiber prevented its degenerating into an aesthetic sentimentalism. Holmes's task as man and national exemplar was colossal. It was no less than to internalize laissez faire. At a time when, as he himself admitted, men could no longer maintain that brittle individualism of each man's doing as he pleased with "his own"; at a time when government was coming itself to own some heretofore private property, operate more, and regulate all; at a time when collectivism was on the march and individualism on the defensive—at such a time Holmes arose and flourished, flourished to change the venue of individuality lest its cause be lost with its case. We seem always to be hearing from his sage voice overtones of admonition like these:

An economy of abundance does not guarantee an economy of happiness. It only makes possible for the resolute a broad enough foundation for the life of the spirit without artificial exclusion of any from it. If you cannot, with the moderns, get what you want, learn,

---

[93] *Collected Legal Papers*, p. 30.     [94] *Ibid.*, p. 31.     [95] *Ibid.*, p. 37.

with the ancient wise, to want what you get. The diminution of wants is as sure a road to happiness as is the augmentation of desires—and a road more sane to those grown sage. Build your personality on intangibles rather than on tangibles; put your pride in a perfection of privacy indefinitely extensible through growth and sharable up to the maximum limit of every artistic effort at communication; identify yourself with the universe; and reap as reward a cosmic sympathy, or at least such human tolerance as constitutes foundation for dynamic peace.

> Love music; love the written word—
> Love things that time will not decay—
> But love not wholly living things
> That death, or life, may bear away.[96]

Through such social distance from impermanence as the poet prescribes, and Holmes's whole life exemplifies, we may be able to save individuality from the death of individualism. To follow this prescription is to internalize the extraversion of laissez faire. It is to become a free man in a world however fated, free to accept one's fate and through that act of acceptance, as Spinoza advised, to transform external fate into internal freedom. There are a few rare spirits, writes Russell Gordon Smith,[97] who, "realizing that life has no meaning save the meaning one gives it, no value save the value one puts upon it, decide that it isn't life that matters but the courage and the laughter one brings to it. These are the Aristocrats."

Such an aristocracy swells the sum of goods to infinity and makes it possible through this expansion for every citizen to possess enough to make him proud. It offers a life of aristocratic fulness within harmonized with a life of lack of utter want without, implemented in their balance by representative authority. By swelling thus the sum of goods aristocracy can be extended to all citizens preserving its ancient spirit in forms

---

[96] Jamie Sexton Holme, *Star Gatherer* (New York: Henry Harrison, 1930), p. 75.

[97] *Fugitive Papers* (New York: Columbia University Press, 1930), p. 118.

modern and democratic. Indeed, a democracy made up of citizens thus wealthy within is in the deepest and truest sense a commonwealth of aristocrats, equal in their rights and immunized by law from the poison of one another's prowess. Since, however, Holmes himself has taught us that it is under the "illusion of self-seeking" called *honor* that most men aspire, let us make democratic honor our final theme. Honor has long been the key word for an aristocratic society; it becomes in the philosophy of this our aristocrat the key word also for the democratic way of life.

### IV. HONOR AS BRIDGE FROM ARISTOCRACY TO DEMOCRACY

Aristocratic in lineage as it is, honor is no less prevalent today, observes Holmes, than in medieval times, when it was supposed to flourish in its fulness.[98] But clearly ours is a transformed conception of honor. It is transformed to fit the evolving world that Holmes foresaw, a world "in which the ideal will be content and dignified acceptance of life, rather than aspiration and the passion for achievement."[99] Life makes its own roads, and from every spot, as Holmes remarks, "there are roads . . . . that will lead you where you will."[100] It is the democratic type of honor which furnishes dynamics for what Holmes speaks of in another connection as "a perfect type of the union of democracy with discipline."[101]

This democratic honor is not an individual ornament to be worn about the neck; it is a collective sacrament to be awarded responsibly. At its most elegant, honor is ambivalent as between those who get and those who give. It takes many a nobody, so to say, to make a somebody. But the nobodies whose deference makes a somebody must themselves be definite somebodies in a democratic state. Otherwise would the somebody made by nobodies become in penalty a puffy no-

---

[98] *Collected Legal Papers*, p. 33.

[99] *Ibid.*, p. 31.

[100] *Ibid.*, p. 31.

[101] *Ibid.*, p. 38.

body. Democratic honor, whose service summoned Holmes to quiet heroism, is, then, a complicated business indeed, with a philosophy all its own. It requires, first, a worthy object; it demands, second, eminent subjects; and it attends, finally, upon the merit of mutuality as between the two.

The object of honor to Holmes was himself, his fellow-men, and, finally, the universe into which he submerged each and all. Whoever could contemplate this progressive and at length vast object without wonder and awe Holmes believed to be not a fit citizen in any realm, for he would be lacking in the potential of a man, in imagination. On the other hand, "if our imagination is strong enough to accept the vision of ourselves as parts inseverable from the rest, and to extend our final interest beyond the boundary of our skins, it justifies the sacrifice even of our lives for ends outside of ourselves."[102] This is the way to grow a self full worthy of respect, for such a self reflects a "beyond" that is nevertheless and still "within." Honor for it becomes altruism without the taint of unction.

Worthy objects must find worthy subjects, as we have said, before democratic honor can ensue and thrive. For honor, we may repeat, is not something simply bequeathed; honor is something jointly created and mutually distributed. Only a craven would be flattered by the plaudits of puling slaves— and yet there are such cravens disgracing high places in the world today. For such personified insults to honor, Gilbert and Sullivan have in the *Gondoliers* applied this salve of sophistry:

> In short, whoever you may be,
> To this conclusion you'll agree
> When every one is somebodee,
> Then no one's anybody.

Seriously imitating this loose logic of comedy, contemporary dictators have before our very eyes tragically reared

[102] *Ibid.*, p. 316.

honor's exact opposite to sit in honor's place. And sitting
there, these pretenders to honor sigh disdainful of the fawning
sea of sycophancy before them; they sigh without the smile
bestowed by our Emily Dickinson upon such conceit:

> How dreary to be somebody.
> How public like a frog,
> To tell your name the livelong day
> To an admiring bog.

When the machinery of mutuality has bogged down in the
terrors of tyranny, the natural yearning of leaders for the
esteem of their fellows is lost in the hollowness which always
intervenes when the barbarism of glory does to the death the
dear institution of honor. Recall Mussolini's boast to Emil
Ludwig that the people "move me no more than this table or
that piece of paper. Among them I am absolutely alone."

Against such pusillanimous braggadocio of the echo-
Caesars of our time, democracy and decency struggle to give
everybody a place on some pyramid of deference so that nobody will become a mere nobody in our civic life. We know
that men must have deference; but we know also that a free
man requires free men to convert approbation into honor.

This insight into mutuality it is which redeems honor from
the racket of totalitarianism and makes of an aristocratic institution a democratic thing indefinitely extensible and inesti-
mably rewarding as between objects and subjects equally
worthy. This it is which makes a homeland of democracy
where only self-respecting equals can feel themselves to be
outwardly free and inwardly clean. Conceit of superiority deadens
honor by cutting away this mutuality of regard. Humility sub-
stitutes pity for honor, letting charity stand for justice until envy
poisons charity. Mutuality, and mutuality alone, founds honor
stably.

This reciprocity of regard is the veritable magic of all civic
morale. For among all things deeply curious and yet infinitely

reassuring about human beings, this I think is most so: that nobody is veritably nobody to himself. Everybody is indeed a somebody to at least onebody. What anyone is to himself he may become to others in a society that is genuinely free. He requires only deference to develop. Important, then, as income is in a competitive society, indispensable as security is in a precarious world, deference is the most prized of all the goods for which and by which men live. But deference must be given in order to be got. This is the secret of democratic honor.

To discover the fecundity of mutuality, as democrats have; to practice the fraternity of the free, the fellowship of the potential, as democrats must—this is to make of competition itself a form of democratic co-operation. Moreover, such mutuality of respect and deference tends to lift life from the level of the competitive to the noncompetitive. It even raises the struggle for deference itself, lethal if left alone with the will-to-power, to the circumspection of justice under the guidance of man's equally ancient will-to-perfection.

As we develop objects of honor made worthy of regard by honoring those who honor them; as we develop subjects of honor made worthy by respecting superiority as a challenge to their own growth—so we develop as the very texture of our citizenship that mutuality of regard which constitutes the inner integrity of our outer life of liberty. As we do this civilized and civilizing thing, we honor our revolutionary heroes like Thomas Paine and promote ourselves to the evolutionary level of Oliver Wendell Holmes, joining thus our aristocratic exemplar in his litany of democratic faith and resolution: "faith in a universe not measured by our fears," [103] resolution that from "seen and unseen powers and destinies of good and evil our trumpets sound once more a note of daring, hope, and will." [104]

[103] *Ibid.*, p. 297.

[104] *Speeches* (Boston: Little, Brown & Co., 1891), p. 12.

# INDEX

✣